SUCCESS

WITH NUMERACY

FOR THE
QTS SKILLS TEST

Les Fairclough, Chris Lea, Rick Nelms, Malcolm Shay

SUCCESS

PUBLICATIONS

Success Publications
The Old School
Chapel Lane
Galgate
Lancs LA2 OPW
Tel: 01942 795494

British Library Cataloguing in Publication Data

Success with Numeracy for the QTS skills test
    1. Mathematics - Examinations, questions, etc.
    I. Fairclough, Les
    510. 7 ' 6

    ISBN 0 9540793 0 2

Acknowledgements

The Authors would like to thank Bob Gallear and students of Nottingham Trent University for pre-testing the written and mental arithmetic questions.
We would also like to thank Siobhan McGuigan for proof reading the manuscript and
Nina Taylor for designing the front cover and CD label.

First published in 2001

Printed for Success Publications by Black Bear Press Limited, Cambridge, England on behalf of The Association for Science Education.

Contents

Introduction

This book and audio CD have been produced as support material for trainee teachers taking the QTS Numeracy Skills Test, first introduced in 2000. The primary aim has been to provide an extensive resource of realistic test questions identical in style and substance to those used in the live test. The materials may be used as part of a Teacher Training course or as a self-study resource.

The contents of this book have been structured to make it versatile and easy to use. The questions, both written and mental, are specifically organised into those aspects of numeracy that are assessed in the test and may be used to develop and practice numeracy skills in those areas. Practice written tests are provided which can be combined with the mental arithmetic tests on the CD or with the mental arithmetic questions in the book. In this way, a variety of tests can be constructed from which the user can gain extensive practice. The audio CD contains seven, timed, mental arithmetic tests that may be used to simulate this aspect of the Numeracy Test.

The book is intended to be used as a workbook and answer boxes have been provided for all the questions. Answer grids are provided in Appendix 2 (pages 110-111). Users can simulate the live test with no more complicated equipment than pencils and CD players. The nature and style of the questions are identical to those in the Numeracy Test. The point and click and drag and drop type questions used in the computer based test are simulated in a written format. The user may access as much or as little of the material as is needed. To facilitate your use of the book, it is provided with a full contents list (page iii) and a comprehensive index (page 112).

Chapter 1 contains an explanation of the nature of the Numeracy Skills Test with details of how to navigate through the test. Examples of the question types are provided along with explanations of each type and advice on how to answer the different question formats.

Chapter 2 deals specifically with the organisation and presentation of data. The aim of this chapter is to familiarise trainee teachers with the ways in which data is recorded, organised and displayed. Examples are provided of how different methods of displaying data are used in a teacher's professional role and how these are used as a basis for test questions. Typical test items are given for each method.

Chapter 3 contains eleven sections, each representing one of the skill areas assessed in the written part of the test. Each section contains eight examples of questions. The first two questions in each section guide the user step by step through the necessary calculations to provide confidence in developing numeracy skills. The other questions can then be used to further develop and practice these skills.

Chapter 4 has seven sections each covering one of the mathematical concepts tested in the mental arithmetic section of the test.

Chapter 5 provides two on-screen (written) practice test sections. These may be used alone or combined with the mental arithmetic questions on the CD to emulate the computerised test.

Chapter 6 contains the answers to all the questions including those on the CD.

The audio CD has seven complete mental arithmetic tests each with an approximate running time of ten minutes. These are identical to those used in the live test and allow the user to gain realistic practice and develop their skills in mental arithmetic.

Chapter 1 The Numeracy Skills Test

This chapter contains some important information about the QTS Numeracy Skills Test with which candidates should be familiar prior to taking the test. Further details and information can be found on the TTA website at **www.canteach.gov.uk.**

The TTA website also provides important information on test registration, booking a test and details of test centres and their locations. Candidates requiring special arrangements can also find details on the TTA website.

Section 1 A Brief Guide to the Test

The Numeracy Skills Test has been designed to ensure that all Newly Qualified Teachers have a basic level of proficiency in numeracy and are able to utilise these skills in their professional role as a teacher. The Test is taken by all trainees seeking Qualified Teacher Status, regardless of their discipline, and it is a requirement of achieving that status that they pass the Numeracy Skills Test. Trainee Teachers will be allowed unlimited attempts at the test.

➢ The test is delivered and marked by computer. Results, recorded as a pass or fail, will be printed out on completion of the test.

➢ The Teacher Training Agency will provide candidates who do not pass the test with feedback outlining their performance on the test. This will allow those candidates who fail the test the opportunity to review those aspects of their numeracy skills that need further work prior to re-sitting the test.

The test is in two sections:

➢ **Section 1** consists of **12 Mental Arithmetic questions** delivered through the computer via headphones.

➢ **Section 2** consists of **16 On-Screen questions** delivered through the computer. Responses to the questions will require the use of the mouse or keyboard.

➢ The normal time allocated for the test is 48 minutes. An on-screen clock allows candidates to keep track of the time during the test.

➢ Candidates with special requirements may be allowed additional time.

➢ The tests are calibrated to be the same standard as the benchmark test (available on **www.canteach.gov.uk**), which has a pass mark of **60%.**

Detailed information on the Mental Arithmetic and the On-Screen sections of the test and examples of the types of questions used in the test can be found in the rest of this chapter.

Section 2 Mental Arithmetic Questions

During this part of the test, you are allowed a piece of paper on which to jot down relevant numbers. Make use of this; you will find it very helpful.

> **You are not permitted to use a calculator for the mental arithmetic section of the test.**

➢ Before the test there will be a practice question.

➢ Each mental arithmetic question will be read **twice.**

➢ Following the second reading, you are allowed **18 seconds** in which to calculate and record your answer. Jot down important numbers during the first or second reading but do not forget the actual question.

➢ You will need to input your answer using the keyboard.

➢ This section of the test does not allow you to go back to a question if you run out of time. If this happens, forget about it and concentrate on the next question.

The mental arithmetic questions will test your ability to carry out mental calculations involving more than one stage, e.g. a multiplication followed by a division.

The context of the questions will be those a teacher would normally meet and use in their professional role. For example, a question might involve a calculation concerning the time allocation for different lesson activities, a process that is a basic part of a teachers' lesson planning.

Processes tested

The questions in this section of the test will require you to carry out mental calculations involving the following:

➢ **time**

➢ **money**

➢ **proportions, fractions and decimals**

➢ **percentages**

➢ **measurements (e.g. distance and area)**

➢ **conversions**

➢ **combinations of the basic processes of addition, subtraction, multiplication and division**

> The audio CD provided with this book contains seven mental arithmetic tests using questions of the same type as used in a live test. Any of these tests may be used in conjunction with the written part of the practice tests in Chapter 5.

Section 3 On-Screen Questions

There are 16 on-screen questions.
All the questions require you to input your answer using either the mouse or the keyboard.

Navigating through the Test

Instructions for the on-screen part of the test are given before the test begins. The instructions give information about the test, the test items and how to move through the test. Read these instructions carefully. The on-screen questions begin immediately after the mental arithmetic questions.

Throughout the test you will meet a number of screen buttons. These are illustrated and explained below.

| next | Click on this to move on to the next question.

| previous | Click here to go back to a question.

| end exam | Clicking this button will bring up a dialogue box asking you to confirm that you wish to end the test. Only click this when you are certain you have finished.

☐ **select for review** Check this box to select a question you wish to view again before the test ends.

| question x | In some questions (the x refers to the question number), you need to click this button to view the question.

| close | Click this to close a question viewed using the button above.

| exhibit | Click this button to view additional information needed to answer the question.

| calculator | Click this to bring up the on-screen calculator. This may be kept open during the test and moved around the screen as necessary.

Diagram illustrating a screen-shot from the Numeracy Test
(Note. Not all of the buttons will be seen at the same time on any one screen)

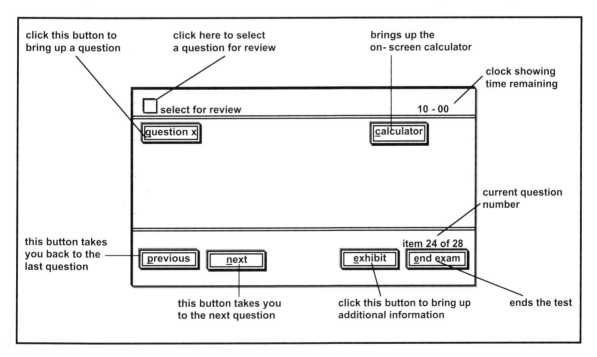

The on-screen clock allows you to keep track of the time remaining.
The screen display shows the number of the question you are attempting.

Question Types

The on-screen part of the test consists of 16 questions in five different formats:

➢ **multiple choice**

➢ **multiple response**

➢ **single response**

➢ **point and click**

➢ **drag and drop**

1. Multiple Choice items

These types of questions will take the following format:

- an introductory statement followed by some form of data, for example, a table, graph or bar chart
- the question
- a number of options or alternative answers (three or four). Only **one** of these (the key) is correct.

To indicate your answer it is necessary to click the circle next to your chosen response. A black dot will appear inside the circle. To change your answer, click on the circle again to cancel the answer and then click on the alternative chosen. In this type of question, the computer will not allow you to indicate more than one response.

An example of a Multiple Choice test item

A class teacher analysed the absences during the autumn term for the five pupils with the worst attendance record in the class. The bar chart shows this analysis.

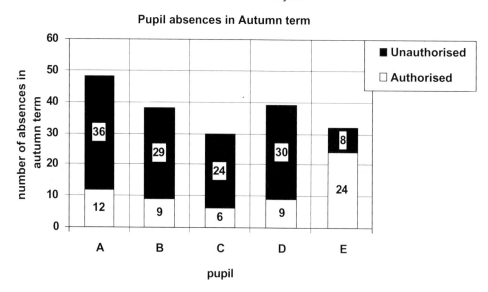

Which pupil had a ratio of authorised absences to unauthorised absences of 1:3?

    ⦿ a. pupil A

    ◯ b. pupil C

    ◯ c. pupil D

In this case, the answer is pupil A with 12 authorised absences and 36 unauthorised absences. This gives a ratio of 12:36 or 1:3 in its simplest form.

2. Multiple Response items

The style of these questions is similar to that of multiple choice:

- an introductory statement
- the data on which the question is based
- the question then provides a number of statements (3 or 4) and you are asked to indicate all the statements that are true.

Unlike multiple choice questions, more than one statement may be correct and you need to consider the validity of each statement independently.

For example, in a question with 3 statements, the following combinations may be possible:

statement 1 only correct
statement 2 only correct
statement 3 only correct
statements 1 and 2 correct
statements 2 and 3 correct
statements 1 and 3 correct
statements 1, 2 and 3 correct

The answer is indicated by clicking on the check box ☐ next to the correct statement or statements. A tick appears in the box or boxes. ☑

Your answer can be changed by clicking on the box again to cancel the tick and then reselecting the answer.

An example of a Multiple Response test item

The table shows the total number of pupils on roll, the number of pupils with Special Educational Needs (SEN) and the number of pupils on free school meals in six Primary schools in a Local Education Authority.

School	Total number of pupils on roll	Number of SEN pupils	Number of pupils on free school meals
A	125	24	32
B	177	30	49
C	144	23	12
D	165	33	33
E	130	26	27
F	210	15	35

Indicate all the true statements:

☑ 1. schools D and E had the same proportion of pupils with Special Educational Needs

☐ 2. 20 % of pupils in School A had Special Educational Needs

☑ 3. school B had the highest proportion of pupils on free school meals

Both statements 1 and 3 are true.

3. Single Response items

As the name suggests, this type of question requires a single answer to be provided using the keyboard. These questions have a similar structure to the previous questions, i.e., an introduction, the data and the question. Normally, the answer will simply be a number. There is no requirement to enter units and a correct answer entered without them will still be scored as correct. If you do choose to enter the unit, always use the correct symbol, for example, **km**. A list of common units and symbols can be found in appendix 1.

Single response questions are the only type used in the Test which allow you a degree of freedom in inputting your answer. The drawback lies in the possible variations in the way a particular answer can be expressed. For example, an answer of **£7.50** can be written as – **7.50, £7,50, £7.50, £7-50p,** and so on. The computer program that scores your answers will have been programmed to accept the most common variations. Avoid unusual formats - your answer may be scored incorrect.

➢ Pay particular attention to the instructions in the question. These tell you how to express your answer. The instructions may, for example, tell you to:
   'give your answer to one decimal place', e.g. **24.6** rather than **24.62**
   'give your answer in its simplest form', e.g. **5:3** not **10:6**
   'give your answer to the nearest pound' e.g. **£18** not **£17.97**
   Answers to one or two decimal places should be rounded up or down as appropriate.

➢ Do not attempt to write your answer in words. If a question asks - 'How many boys achieved Level 5?' and the answer is '**7**', type '**7**' rather than '**7 boys**'. Although this latter answer would be marked correct, any typing error would lose you the mark.

➢ Take care with answers requiring a monetary value as the answer.
   An answer of '**£10.58**' should not be written with spaces as '**£10 58**' or '**£10 58**'. Use a full stop (**.**) or a dash (**-**) between the pounds and pence.

➢ Answers in terms of time also need care in their expression. Always use the twenty-four hour clock.
   An answer of '**9.15**' a.m. should be written as '**09-15**', '**09:15**', '**0915**' or '**09.15**'.
   An answer of '**7 o'clock**' in the evening should be written as '**19-00**', 19:00, '**1900**' or 19.00.

An example of a Single Response test item

Table 1 shows the GCSE points score for each grade.
Table 1

GCSE Grade	A*	A	B	C	D	E	F	G	U
Points score	8	7	6	5	4	3	2	1	0

A pupil took six GCSE examinations in the subjects shown in Table 2 and achieved the grades listed.

Table 2

GCSE Subject	Grade achieved
English	A
Mathematics	C
Science	D
History	C
Geography	E
Music	

The pupil's mean GCSE points score from the 6 subjects was 4.5.
What grade did the pupil achieve in Music?

The answer to this question is simply a letter, in this case - '**E**'.
Note: there is no need to type in '**grade E**'.

4. Point and Click items

This style of question requires you to point with the mouse and click on one or more items of data or points in a table, graph or chart. Clicking on a point will cause a circle to appear. If you make a mistake, you can change your answer by clicking again on the point to cancel it and then clicking on the correct point. Normally, but not always, such questions will indicate the number of answers or clicks required.

An example of a Point and Click test item

The previous question can be used as an illustration of a point and click question.

Table 1 shows the GCSE point scores for each grade.

Table 1

GCSE Grade	A*	A	B	C	D	E ⊗	F	G	U
Point score	8	7	6	5	4	3	2	1	0

A pupil took six GCSE examinations in the subjects shown in Table 2 and achieved the grades listed.

Table 2

GCSE Subject	Grade achieved
English	A
Mathematics	C
Science	D
History	C
Geography	E
Music	

The pupil's mean GCSE points score from the 6 subjects was 4.5.

Click in Table 1 on the GCSE grade the pupil achieved in Music.

The answer is indicated by clicking on grade 'E' in Table 1 (as shown by the ⊗ in the table).

The data and the answer are identical in this example and the previous one. It is only the way in which the question is asked and the method of responding which is different.

The instructions for answering point and click items in the Test tell you to **click** (with the mouse) on specified locations on the computer screen. In this book, the process is simulated by instructions telling you to **circle** around specified locations on the page.

5. Drag and Drop items

In a drag and drop question the answer is selected from a series of alternatives. These alternatives are presented in boxes. The box containing the correct answer is dragged using the mouse and dropped into the correct position in a table or chart.

You need to click on the box containing your chosen answer and holding the mouse button down move the box to the correct position. Releasing the mouse button will cause the box to drop into the chosen position in the chart or table.

You can change your answer by dragging it out of the table and back to its original position. Reselect your answer and move it in the same way.

An example of a Drag and Drop test item

The table shows the percentage of pupils achieving Level 4 and above in end of Key Stage 3 English, Mathematics and Science between 1996 and 2000 and the mean for the 5 years for each subject.

	Percentage of pupils achieving Level 4 and above in end of Key Stage 3		
Year	English	Mathematics	Science
1996	36	39	41
1997	33	37	39
1998	39	40	40
1999	place here	41	44
2000	42	46	43
Mean	36.6	place here	41.4

Select and place the correct value in the boxes to complete the table.

33		34		35

40.1		40.6		41.6

The percentage for English in 1999 is [33] and this box would be moved and dropped into the correct box in the table.

The mean for Mathematics is [40.6] and this box would be moved and dropped into the correct box in the table.

The instructions for answering drag and drop items in the Test tell you to **select** and **place** the answer(s) (with the mouse) into answer boxes on the computer screen. In this book, the process is simulated by instructions telling you to **select** and **write** the answer(s) into the shaded boxes.

Processes tested

The on-screen part of the test covers two aspects of numeracy:

1. Interpreting and using statistical information involving:

➢ the identification of trends correctly

➢ making comparisons in order to draw conclusions

➢ interpreting information accurately.

2. Using and applying general arithmetic involving the concepts of:

➢ time

➢ money

➢ proportion and ratio

➢ percentages, fractions and decimals

➢ measurements (e.g. distance and area)

➢ conversions (e.g. from one currency to another, from fractions to decimals or percentages)

➢ averages (including mean, median, mode and range where relevant)

➢ simple given formulae

> **Chapter 3 contains a large number of practice test questions giving extensive coverage of each of these aspects of numeracy.**

QUALIFIED TEACHER STATUS NUMERACY SKILLS TEST - SUMMARY	
Delivery	By computer
Time	48 minutes
Questions	28
1. Mental arithmetic	12
2. On-screen	16

Chapter 2 Data Presentation

Many of the questions in the Numeracy Skills Test are designed to test your ability to analyse and interpret statistical information. Data on which the Test questions are based will be presented in a variety of forms: tables, bar charts, pie charts, line graphs, cumulative frequency graphs, scatter graphs and box and whisker diagrams. You will be familiar with many of these but some may be unfamiliar. These methods of organising and displaying data are ones teachers meet and use on a regular basis in carrying out their normal, professional duties and are ones encountered in official statistics from such bodies as Local Education Authorities, the DfES and QCA. Teachers record, organise and display information on an everyday basis. Class registers, mark books and lesson plans are records kept daily. Being able to manipulate, record and present data is a valuable teaching tool and an understanding of data handling will help improve your effectiveness as a teacher.

How data is arranged and presented depends on the type of information and its intended use. Raw data such as pupil's test marks is a record best kept in a simple table, of which a mark book is a good example. If the purpose is to compare information such as examination results for different classes, it is useful to process the data into percentages and a bar chart may be a more appropriate method of displaying this type of data. A line graph would be an appropriate way of comparing similar information, such as the percentage of GCSE grades A* - C in a subject over several years.

The aim of this chapter is to show the various ways in which statistics are presented and displayed in the Numeracy Test and to familiarise you with these. Each method of presenting data is followed by a sample question to provide practice in analysing and interpreting information. The answers are on page 26.

1 Tables

The purpose of tabulating data is to present it in a form which is clear and can be read quickly and easily. Tabulation involves arranging the information in a series of rows and columns, the number of which depends on the complexity of the data. Tables are usually the primary method used to organise and present information and are the form with which you will be most familiar. The Numeracy Test makes extensive use of tabulated data as question sources.

Tables are easy to construct and can be used for most types of records. In a teaching context, these may be pupil's attendance, pupil's test marks, end of Key Stage test results, examination results and stock records. Tables can be used to record data for a single group such as test marks for pupils in one class, or for comparative purposes such as marks in the same test for a range of classes or over a period of time. A spreadsheet is an example of a table. When reading tables in the test, study the headings carefully as the question often relates to only part of the information, especially in tables containing a large amount of data.

Example 1

This example is a simple table with only five items of information.

The table shows the weekly attendance for five classes.

Class	A (20 pupils)	B (24 pupils)	C (23 pupils)	D (22 pupils)	E (19 pupils)
Weekly attendance (Maximum of 10 for an individual pupil)	180	232	220	218	177

Select and place the correct percentage in the box underneath the class with the best attendance record. (To simulate the drag and drop write the answer in the correct box above)

99.1%	96.7%	95.6%	93.0%

Example 2

This example of a tabulated record is more complex than the previous one and contains twelve items of information concerned with the GCSE entry for English in a school and the number of pupils achieving a range of grades.

The table shows the number of pupils in a school entered for GCSE English and the number achieving GCSE grades A*- C and A*- G from 1997 to 2000.

		GCSE results in English	
Year	Entry	Number achieving A* - C	Number achieving A* - G
1997	178	90	171
1998	175	85	165
1999	161	82	152
2000	169	96	163

In which two years did more than 95% of pupils achieve grades A* - G?

☐ a. 1997 and 1998

☐ b. 1997 and 1999

☐ c. 1997 and 2000

☐ d. 1999 and 2000

Example 3

This example is even more complex. The two main columns have been sub-divided to give additional information about the gender of pupils admitted to and leaving a school.

The table shows the number of pupils admitted to a school and the number of pupils leaving the school each year from 1994 to 1999.

	Number admitted to the school		Number leaving the school	
School Year	Boys	Girls	Boys	Girls
1994	140	155	95	85
1995	148	152	125	75
1996	147	155	130	120
1997	160	145	135	95
1998	140	135	138	122
1999	145	122	139	156

Indicate all the true statements:

☐ 1. in 1998, 15 more pupils were admitted than left the school

☐ 2. the number of pupils leaving the school increased every year

☐ 3. in 1996, 52 % of pupils leaving were boys

☐ 4. in 1997, the number of pupils in the school increased by 77

Example 4

This example is a very complex table containing 108 items of information. This type of table is one frequently used in official documents such as the Autumn package from the DfES. You are unlikely to meet a more complicated example in the Numeracy Test.

The table shows the percentage of pupils, in a school and nationally, achieving different Levels in end of Key Stage 2 English, Mathematics and Science.

(N= National figures, S = School figures)

	Percentage of pupils achieving different Levels in end of Key Stage 2																	
	English						Mathematics						Science					
	Boys		Girls		Total		Boys		Girls		Total		Boys		Girls		Total	
Level	N	S	N	S	N	S	N	S	N	S	N	S	N	S	N	S	N	S
1	1	5	1	3	1	4	1	2	1	4	1	3	1	6	1	5	1	6
2	8	16	4	12	6	13	6	7	5	6	6	7	4	10	3	8	4	9
3	31	45	23	31	27	38	28	33	28	33	28	33	24	28	23	27	24	28
4	45	28	50	40	48	34	44	48	49	49	47	48	51	50	55	53	53	51
5	13	5	22	13	17	9	19	10	17	8	18	9	19	5	17	6	18	6
6	0	0	0	0	0	0	0	0	0	0	0	0	0	0	0	0	0	0

(percentages may not add up to 100 due to rounding)

Click on the letter of the column (A, B, C or D) in the table below, that correctly shows both the percentage of pupils at the school gaining Level 4 and above in Mathematics and the percentage of girls, nationally, gaining Level 4 and above in English.
(To simulate the point and click, circle the correct letter (A, B, C or D in the table below)

	A	B	C	D
Percentage of pupils at the school gaining Level 4 and above in Mathematics	56	65	57	71
Percentage of girls, nationally, gaining Level 4 and above in English	72	73	72	59

Two way Tables

Example 5

This type of table is used to allow direct comparison to be made between two independent sets of data. In the example shown below, the end of Key Stage 3 Levels and the GCSE grades for the same group of sixty pupils have been recorded. It is possible to compare the end of Key Stage 3 level obtained by pupils with their GCSE grade obtained two years later. For example, two pupils who achieved Level 8 also achieved GCSE grade A* and six pupils who achieved Level 4 also achieved GCSE grade E – these are shown shaded in the table.

The table shows the end of Key Stage 3 and GCSE results in English for a group of sixty pupils.

	GCSE grade in English							
	G	**F**	**E**	**D**	**C**	**B**	**A**	**A***
3	5	5	2					
4	3	3	6	2	2			
5	2		2	1	7	2		
6					6	1		
7					2	1	1	
8					2	1	2	2

(row labels under "English end of Key Stage 3 Level")

What proportion of the pupils achieved Level 5 and above in end of Key Stage 3 English and achieved GCSE grade C or better?
Give your answer as a decimal.

Example 6

This two way table has been constructed to compare reading age with actual age.

The table shows the actual age and reading age for thirty Year 5 pupils.

		Reading age in years and months											
Y	**M**	9 0	9 1	9 2	9 3	9 4	9 5	9 6	9 7	9 8	9 9	9 10	9 11
9	0	1	1										
9	1												
9	2								1				
9	3				2			1					
9	4		2			1		1	1				
9	5			1			1						1
9	6				1					1			1
9	7			1				2	1		1	1	
9	8									1			
9	9										1	1	
9	10				1	1		1		1			
9	11												

(row labels under "Actual age in years and months")

What percentage of pupils had a reading age 3 months or more above than their actual age?

2 Charts

The two most frequently used types of chart are Bar Charts and Pie Charts. Both provide a pictorial method of displaying information and it is often easier to analyse data when it is presented in these forms rather than in a table.

A Bar Charts

Bar charts are an ideal way of presenting data in a clear and visual form and have a variety of uses in a teaching context including keeping records of attendance, pupil performance such as examination and test results and their direct use in teaching situations.

The data that is to be plotted is organised into distinct categories such as years, classes, year groups, GCSE grades and end of Key Stage Levels. Each category is plotted along the horizontal (x) axis. The quantity or value, which may be numbers, percentages or proportions, is plotted on the vertical (y) axis. Simple bar charts have only a single set of data relating to each category while more complex bar charts may have several sets of data. Examples of both these types are given below.

Example 1

The table shows the number of pupils in a class achieving different Levels in end of Key Stage 3 mathematics.

	Number of pupils achieving different Levels in end of Key Stage 3 Mathematics					
Level	Level 3	Level 4	Level 5	Level 6	Level 7	Level 8
Number of pupils	3	3	7	5	6	6

The information in this table can be represented as a simple bar chart. In this example, the categories are the end of Key Stage 3 Levels (plotted on the horizontal axis) and the value is the number of pupils (plotted on the vertical axis). The use of a bar chart makes it easy to make a visual comparison between the numbers of pupils achieving each Level.

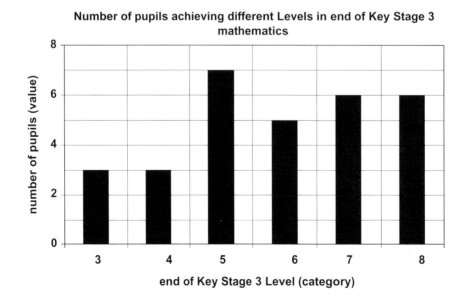

Number of pupils achieving different Levels in end of Key Stage 3 mathematics

Example 2

The bar chart shows the mean test History scores test for boys and girls in five classes. This example has two sets of data (boys and girls) in each category.

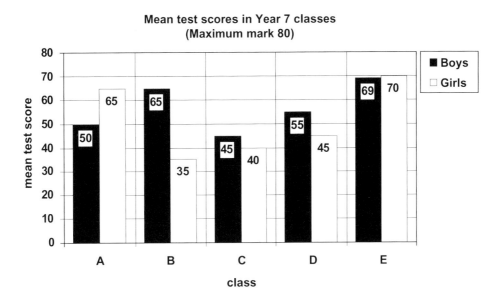

Indicate all the true statements:

1. the range of mean test scores for girls across the five classes was 33

2. in classes B and E, the mean test score for boys was more than 80% of the maximum test score

3. the girls gained higher mean test scores than the boys in more than half the classes

Example 3

The bar chart shows the total number of 1/2 day absences for three classes in three terms.
This is an example of a stacked bar chart. The total number of 1/2 day absences for each class, in each term, are shown stacked on top of each other.

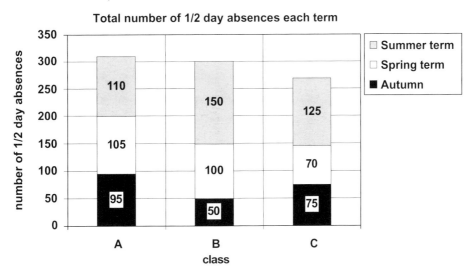

In which class were the absences for the Summer term 50 % of the total absences for the year?

B Pie Charts

Pie charts are a diagrammatic way of showing how a group is divided up into different parts. They also show the proportion of the whole, each part represents. The bigger the proportion, the bigger the 'slice' of the 'pie'. In example 1 below, the pie is the total number of pupils and the slices are the numbers at each Level.

Example 1

This table shows the number of pupils in a class achieving different Levels in end of Key Stage 3 English.

	Number of pupils achieving different Levels in end of Key Stage 3 English					
Level	3	4	5	6	7	8
Number of pupils	4	4	9	7	4	2

This information can be represented pictorially as a pie chart. There are thirty pupils. Level 5 has the biggest proportion, nine pupils, and therefore has the biggest 'slice' of the pie. Levels 3 and 4 have equal numbers of pupils and have equal 'slices'.

Number of pupils achieving different Levels in end of Key Stage 3 English

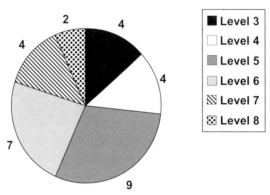

Example 2

The pie chart shows the intended destinations of 70 Primary school pupils at the end of year 6.

Destinations of Year 6 pupils

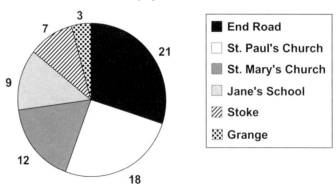

Indicate all the true statements:

1. End Road school was the destination for 32 % of the pupils

2. a Church school was the destination for 2/5 of the pupils

3. End Road school was the destination of 3 times more pupils than Stoke

Example 3

The pie chart shows the number of pupils in a school choosing different activities during a sports day involving all 1104 pupils.

Number of pupils choosing different activities

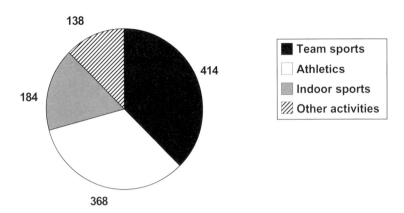

The table shows the fraction of children choosing options at the sports day from 1998 to 2000.

	1998	1999	2000
Team sports	2/5	1/3	3/8
Athletics	1/3	1/4	1/3
Indoor sports	1/6	1/6	1/6
Other activities	1/5	1/8	1/8

Which year is shown by the pie chart?

Example 4

180 pupils in a school took the GCSE English examination. The pie chart shows the proportion of pupils achieving each grade.

Proportion of pupils achieving each grade

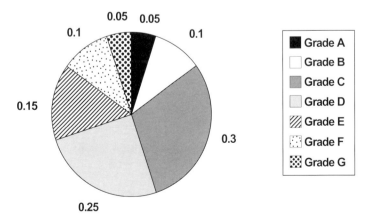

How many pupils achieved grades A – C?

3 Graphs

A Line Graphs

Most of the data represented in a bar chart may be shown as a line graph provided the quantity on the horizontal (x) axis is continuous, for example, time. In a line graph the data is plotted as a series of points that are joined by a straight or curved line.

Line graphs are particularly useful in showing a trend over a period of time. This may be, for example, the number of GCSE grades A* - G in a subject over a number of years, the numbers of pupils enrolling at a school over several years or the number of absences in a class or Year group over a year. Although such information can be shown as a bar chart, line graphs give a better visual representation of any patterns in the data. An example is given below.

Example 1

A school introduced an initiative to reduce absences in a year group. This commenced at the start of week 7 of a 10-week term.
The table shows the percentage absences in the year group over the term.

End of week	1	2	3	4	5	6	7	8	9	10
% absences	4.8	5.2	6.0	6.4	6.6	7.0	6.2	5.0	4.8	4.4

This data has been plotted as a line graph.

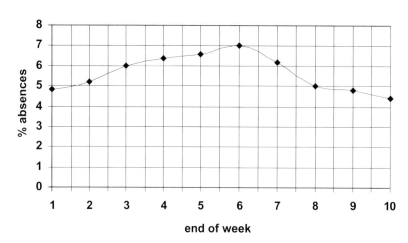

Percentage absences over a ten week period

The use of a line graph, in this context, makes it easy to see that the trend in the absence pattern rises over the first 6 weeks and then falls from the start of week 7 onwards. The school could use the information in the graph to monitor the effects of its initiative on the number of absences.

A similar line graph could be drawn showing the absences for several year groups. This would have different lines for each year group. Similarly, a line graph can be used to show, for example, the proportion of pupils achieving a given Level and above in end of Key Stage tests or for comparison of a school's examination results with other schools or with national figures over a number of years.

Example 2

The graph shows pupil admissions to the Reception classes of three Primary schools from 1996 to 2000.

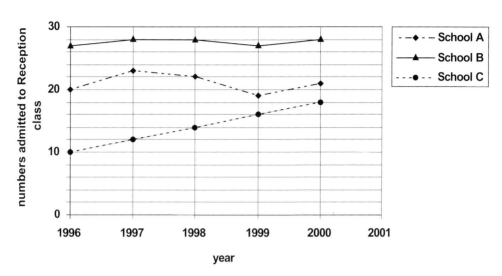

Numbers admitted to Reception class. 1996 - 2000

Indicate all the true statements:

1. the greatest difference in the admissions to school A and school B was in 1996

2. in 1996, the admissions to school C were half of the admissions to school A

3. if the trend continues, admissions to school C will be 20 in 2001

Example 3

The graph shows the percentage of pupils in a school achieving GCSE grades A* - G and grades A* - C in French from 1996 to 2000.

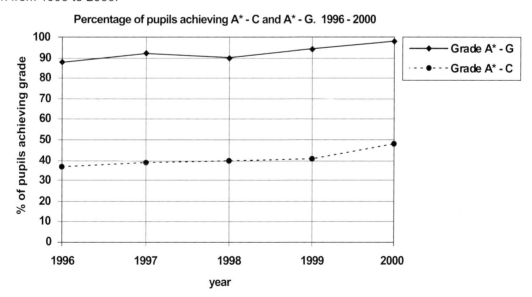

Percentage of pupils achieving A* - C and A* - G. 1996 - 2000

What percentage of pupils achieved less than grade C in 1998?

B Cumulative Frequency Graphs

Frequency is the number of times an event or value occurs. This could be, for example, the numbers of pupils achieving end of Key Stage 3 Levels in a class. Cumulative frequency is the total frequency up to a particular value. Cumulative means to increase by successive additions.

Example 1

The table shows a school's end of Key Stage 3 test results in English.

	English end of Key Stage 3 Levels	
Level	Number of pupils (Frequency)	Cumulative frequency
N	10	10
3	20	30 (10 + 20)
4	25	55 (30 + 25)
5	35	90 (55 + 35)
6	50	140 (90 + 50)
7	30	170 (140 + 30)
8	10	180 (170 + 10)
Total	180	180

The second column of the table shows the number of pupils (**frequency**) achieving each Level.
The third column shows the **cumulative frequency**. This is obtained by adding each frequency to the sum of the previous ones. For example, the cumulative frequency at Level 4 (**55**) is obtained by adding the frequency at Level 4 (**25**) to the total of the previous Levels (**30**). Effectively, the cumulative frequency is a running total. From the table it can be easily seen that 90 pupils achieved Level 5 or below.
i.e. **10** pupils at N + **20** pupils at Level 3 + **25** pupils at Level 4 + **35** pupils at Level 5 = **90** pupils.

To convert this information into a graph, **cumulative frequencies** (not the frequency) are plotted against the **Levels**. Cumulative frequency is always plotted on the vertical (y) axis.
So 10 pupils are plotted against Level N, 30 pupils against Level 3, 55 pupils against Level 4 and so on.

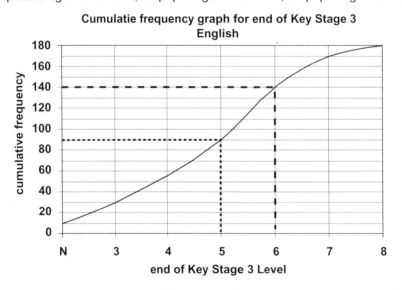

Graphs of this type allow such questions as "What percentage of pupils achieved Level 7 and above?" to be answered. To answer this question the number of pupils who achieved Level 6 and below (– – – –) is read from the graph. This is 140 pupils. The total number of pupils is 180, therefore, the number of pupils achieving Level 7 and above is 180 – 140 = 40. The next step is to convert this to a percentage using the formula: Percentage = 40 ÷ 180 x 100 = 22.2 rounded down to 22 % of pupils
This graph can also be used to find the **median**. The median Level is the Level achieved by the middle pupil. There are 180 pupils, so the middle pupil is the 90th. Read across from 90 on the vertical axis (••••••••) to the line, then read down to the Level. In this case, the median is Level 5.

Example 2

A Primary school surveyed the distances travelled to school by its 240 pupils.
The results of the survey are shown in the cumulative frequency graph.

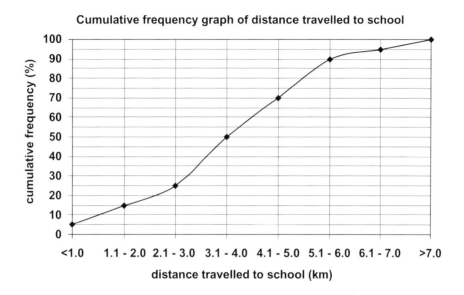

Cumulative frequency graph of distance travelled to school

Select and write the correct value in the box to show the number of pupils travelling more than 5.0 km to school.

| 24 | 30 | 72 |

The number of pupils travelling more than 5.0 km to school is

C Scatter Graphs

The charts and graphs illustrated so far have all been concerned with one independent variable, for example, the number of GCSE grades A* - C or the number of absences. Some statistical information concerns two independent variables. These two variables may have a correlation or relationship and are often represented in a scatter graph. This provides a visual representation of the data and makes it easy to see if a relationship does exist between the two sets of data. The example below shows the test marks achieved by a group of pupils in two tests in the same subject.

Example 1

Pupil	A	B	C	D	E	F	G	H	I	J
% mark in Test 1	10	28	36	42	50	55	70	72	80	90
% mark in Test 2	10	30	48	80	35	58	50	72	70	90

This data has been plotted on the scatter graph below.

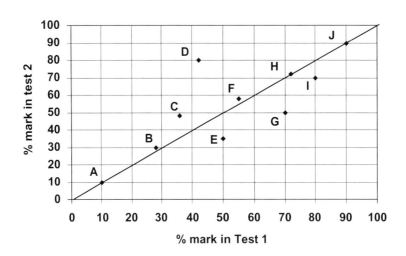

Scatter graph showing marks in Test 1 and Test 2

The line on the graph represents the correlation between the two sets of data. Pupils whose points lie on this line (**A, H** and **J**) have achieved the same mark in both tests. Pupils whose points are above this line (**B, C, D and F**) scored a better mark in Test 2 than in Test 1 and pupils whose points lie below this line (**E, G** and **I**) scored a higher mark in Test 1 than in Test 2.

If the points on a scatter graph are scattered randomly with no apparent pattern there is likely to be little or no relationship between the two sets of data. If the points lie close to the line and form a regular pattern there is likely to be a close relationship.

Graphs of this type allow us to answer such questions as "How many pupils scored higher marks in Test 1 than in Test 2?" or "What proportion of the pupils achieved the same mark in both tests?"

Analysis of the graph allows a teacher to spot individual pupils who might be under-performing. In the example above, pupil D scored highly in Test 2 but considerably less well in Test 1. Similarly, if a scatter graph revealed that most pupils in a class scored highly in one test but poorly in a second test, it may raise the question, "Was the second test of a higher level of difficulty than the first test?" Scatter graphs are particularly useful for representing information about pupil's reading age compared to their actual age and provide a valuable tool for analysing such data.

Example 2

A teacher prepared a scatter graph of the results in spelling and mental arithmetic tests for Year 4 pupils.

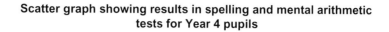

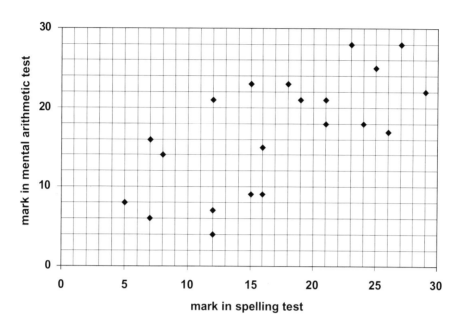

The teacher summarised the key points from the scatter graph in a table, part of which is shown below.

(1)	pupils gained more than 20 marks on both tests
(2)	pupils gained less than 10 marks on the mental arithmetic test
(3)	pupils gained less than 10 marks on both tests

Select and write the correct values in the boxes **(1)**, **(2)** and **(3)** to complete the table.

4 Box and Whisker Diagrams

These are a way of presenting groups of data in a graphical format, with each group of data being represented as a box and whisker diagram on the graph. To analyse and interpret box and whisker diagrams you need to be familiar with the terms, median, range, upper and lower quartiles and inter-quartile range.

Box and whisker diagrams are best explained using an example.

Example 1

The History test marks for a group of twenty eight pupils are arranged in order from lowest to highest.

5 5 6 7 8 10 11 12 14 17 19 20 20 $\boxed{21\ 23}$ 24 24 24 25 26 27 28 29 30 31 34 35 37

➢ The **median** mark is the mark above and below which half or fifty percent of the pupil's marks lie. It can also be described as the middle value of the distribution of marks. The example has two middle values, 21 and 23, (shaded above), therefore the median is the mean of 21 and 23 i.e. **22**. Fourteen of the 28 pupils scored less than 22 marks and 14 pupils scored above 22.

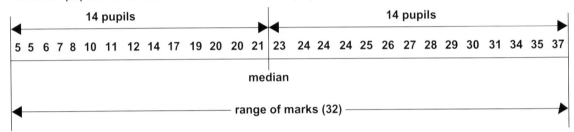

➢ The **range** of marks is the difference between the highest mark and the lowest mark. In this example, the highest mark is 37 and the lowest is 5. Therefore the range is 37 – 5 = 32 marks.

➢ The **lower quartile** is the mark or value below which one quarter or twenty five percent of the marks lie. In this example, the lower quartile is 12 marks. A quarter of the 28 pupils i.e. 7 of the pupils scored less than 12 marks.

➢ The **upper quartile** is the mark or value above which one quarter or twenty five percent of the marks lie. In this example, the upper quartile is 27 marks. A quarter of the 28 pupils i.e. 7 pupils scored more than 27 marks.

➢ The **inter-quartile range** is the range of marks within which half or fifty percent of pupils lie. In this example, the inter-quartile range is 12 marks to 27 marks. Half of the 28 pupils i.e. 14 pupils scored in this range.

The diagram illustrates these terms.

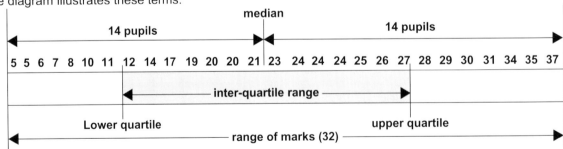

A box and whisker diagram can now be constructed using this information. A box is drawn around the middle fifty percent (**the inter-quartile range**) of marks. The box shows the range of marks (12 to 27) between the **lower quartile** and the **upper quartile**. A line across the box shows the median mark. Whiskers extend from the centre of the box to the highest and lowest marks.

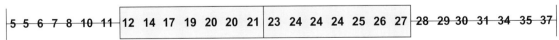

The ends of the two whiskers show the highest and lowest marks in the range (5 to 37).

Normally, box and whisker diagrams are drawn onto a grid as shown below.

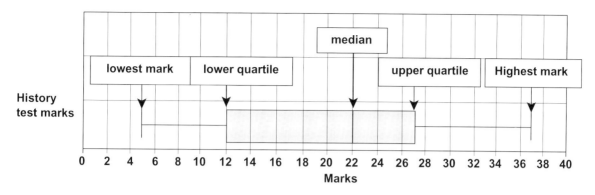

Box and whisker diagrams may be drawn horizontally, as above, or vertically. Several box and whisker diagrams may be drawn side by side to compare, for example, the test results for different classes.

Example 2

A Secondary school teacher prepared a box and whisker diagram to show the range of marks achieved by a tutor group in the end of term tests in five subjects.

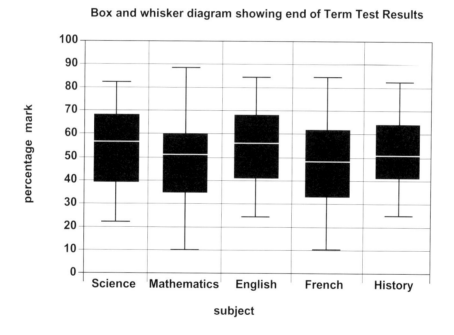

Indicate all the true statements:

	1. the median mark was less than 50 % in one of the 5 subjects
	2. the range of marks was greatest in Maths
	3. the inter-quartile range was the same in Science and English

Answers to questions in this Chapter

Section	Answer	Explanation
Tables **Example 1**	Class D 99.1 %	Maximum possible attendance for class D = 220. 218 ÷ 220 x 100 = 99.09 % rounded up to 99.1 % Class A = 90.0 %. Class B = 96.7 % Class C = 95.6 %. Class E = 93.0 %
Example 2	c	1997 = 171 ÷ 178 x 100 = 96.1 % 2000 = 163 ÷ 169 x 100 = 96.4 %
Example 3	1 and 3 are true	Statement 1 Total admitted in 1998 = 275 Total leaving = 260. Difference = 15 Statement 3 Total pupils leaving = 250 Number of boys = 130. % of boys = 130 ÷ 250 x 100 = 52 %
Example 4	C	% of pupils at school achieving Level 4 and above in mathematics = 48 + 9 = 57 % % of girls nationally achieving Level 4 and above in English = 50 + 22 = 72 %
Example 5	0.45	Total pupils = 60. GCSE grade C or better = 29, of whom 27 achieved Level 5. Proportion achieving Level 5 and grade C or better = 27 ÷ 60 = 0.45
Example 6	20 %	Total number of pupils = 30. Pupils with a reading age 3 months above actual age = 6 Percentage = 6 ÷ 30 x 100 = 20 %
Bar charts **Example 2**	2 is true	Statement 2 Total marks = 80 80% of 80 = 80 ÷ 100 x 80 = 64 marks Mean for boys in class B = 65, mean in class E = 69
Example 3	Class B	Total yearly absences for class B = 300. Absences for Summer term = 150. 150 ÷ 300 = 1/2
Pie charts **Example 2**	3 is true	Statement 3 21 pupils going to End Road school. 7 pupils going to Stoke school. Therefore 3 times more to End Road
Example 3	2000	Total pupils = 1104. Team sports = 414. 1/8 of 1104 = 138 Therefore 3/8 = 138 x 3 = 414 Athletics = 368. 1/3 of 1104 = 368 Indoor sports = 184. 1/6 of 1104 = 184 other activities = 138. 1/8 of 1104 = 138
Example 4	81	Total pupils = 180. Grades A – C = 0.45. 180 x 0.45 = 81
Line graphs **Example 2**	2 and 3 are true	Statement 2 School C admissions in 1996 were 10. School A admissions were 20 Statement 3 Trend for school C is an increase of 2 per year Admissions in 2001 will be 20 if trend continues
Example 3	50 %	Grades A* - G in 1998 = 90 %. Grades A*- C = 40 % Less than grade C = 90 – 40 = 50 %
Cumulative frequency graphs **Example 2**	72	% of pupils travelling up to 5 km = 70. Therefore 30 % travel more than 5 km. Total pupils = 240 30 % of 240 = 30 x 240 ÷ 100 = 72 pupils
Scatter graphs **Example 2**	Box 1 = 5 Box 2 = 6 Box 3 = 2	Box 1 = 5 Draw a line from 20 on both axes. 5 pupils are above and to right of the intersection Box 2 = 6 Draw a line across from 10 on vertical axis. 6 pupils are below this line Box 3 = 2 Draw a line from 10 on both axes. 2 pupils are below and to left of the intersection
Box and whisker diagrams **Example 2**	1 and 2 are true	Statement 1 Median is shown by the line across the box. Line is below 50 % in French only Statement 2 Range of marks is shown by the line from whisker to whisker. Longest line is in Mathematics Therefore Mathematics has the greatest range

Chapter 3 Skills Practice - Written

The purpose of this chapter is to provide you with an extensive resource of pre-tested questions with which to develop your numeracy skills prior to taking the QTS Numeracy Test. The questions have been constructed to mirror the style and format of those used in the live test and have been tested by Trainee Teachers. The chapter is organised into sections, each covering one of the aspects of numeracy with which you are expected to be familiar. This arrangement enables you to go straight to the area(s) with which you feel less confident and to use the questions to gain practice and experience. Use the contents list and index to find specific topics and types of question.

Each section begins with two **Step by Step questions**. These questions have been broken down into the steps or stages required to arrive at the answer. Working through the steps suggested guides you to the answer and shows you the processes that can be used to answer other questions. This will help you to gain confidence in answering the types of questions you will meet in the live tests. These Step by Step questions show only one of the possible routes to the answer. You should realise that there are often several ways of approaching a problem.

Following the Step by Step questions there are six further examples of **Skills Practice questions** to provide more training in each aspect of numeracy. These will enable you to put into practice the skills that you have developed from the Step by Step questions. You should aim to do as many of the Skills Practice questions as possible, particularly in those areas in which you are less confident. The answers to all the questions can be found in Chapter 6.

Many candidates find the on-screen part of the test less demanding than the mental arithmetic. There is less pressure of time, and you have the opportunity to leave a question and go back to it later.

Tips for answering the questions:

➢ read the questions carefully

➢ make sure you understand what the question is asking

➢ keep an eye on the time. You should aim to answer each question in about two minutes

➢ if you don't understand or the question is taking too long, go on to the next one. You can go back to it later

➢ work through logically to the answer

➢ for multiple choice questions, work out the correct answer, and click only **one** alternative (in the book, tick the box)

➢ for multiple response questions, evaluate each response separately, and click on it only if correct (in the book, tick the box or boxes). One or more of the responses may be correct

➢ for single response questions, work out the right answer, and type it in as instructed (in the book, write in the answer box)

➢ for point and click questions, work out the correct answer(s) and click as instructed in the question (in the book, circle the answer or answers)

➢ for drag and drop questions, work out the correct answers(s) and select and place as indicated (in the book, write in the space or spaces).

Interpreting and Using Statistical Information

Section 1 Identify Trends correctly

Step by Step Question 1

A teacher analysed the mean test results obtained by three classes in a series of spelling tests. Each spelling test had a maximum mark of twenty.

	Test 1	Test 2	Test 3	Test 4	Test 5
Class A	10.1	10.3	10.7	10.9	
Class B	6.7	7.4	8.1	8.8	
Class C	7.3	8.7	9.9	10.8	

What will be the mean test result for Class B in Test 5, if present trends continue?

☐ a. 8.8

☐ b. 9.2

☐ c. 9.5

Step by step calculation

In this question you are required to use the information in the table to work out a mean increase. Use the boxes next to each step to write your answers.

To find the trend for class B

Step 1 Find the trend by subtracting the mean of each test from the next test mark in sequence, e.g. test 1 from test 2, test 2 from test 3, etc.
Do all the subtractions give the same answer?

Step 2 Add the result from step 1 to the mean score of test 4 for class B

Put a tick in the box next to the correct answer

Step by Step Question 2

The table gives some information about two Primary schools.

Year	Number of pupils admitted		End of Key Stage 2 mean points score		% of pupils receiving free school meals	
	School A	School B	School A	School B	School A	School B
1997	15	19	20.6	18.7	10	15
1998	16	21	22.1	20.2	8	16
1999	17	23	22.5	20.6	12	15
2000	18	25	24.7	22.6	13	18

Indicate all the true statements:

1. over the four year period, admissions to school B increased twice as fast as admissions to school A

2. in both schools, the proportion of pupils receiving free school meals increased by 30 % between 1997 and 2000

3. the difference between the end of Key Stage 2 mean points score of the two schools was the same each year

Step by step calculation

In this question you are required to compare information to work out trends and differences. You are also required to subtract some of the values and to work out percentages. Use the boxes next to each step to write your answers.

To find out if admissions to school B increased twice as fast as admissions to school A

Step 1 Look at the admissions data for school A. What is the increase per year?

per year

Step 2 Look at the admissions data for school B. What is the increase per year?

per year

Step 3 Have the admissions to school B increased twice as fast as those for school A?

Tick the box if statement 1 is correct

To find the percentage increase in the proportion of pupils receiving free school meals

Step 1 Find the percentage increase in School A. Use the formula:
Percentage increase = (difference in numbers between 2000 and 1997 ÷ number in 1997) x 100

%

Step 2 Find the percentage increase in School B using the same formula as above

%

Tick the box if statement 2 is correct

To find the difference in the end of Key Stage 2 points score for the two schools in each year

Step 1 Find the difference in 1997 by subtracting the lower number (school B) from the higher number (school A).

1997 =

Step 2 Repeat the same arithmetical process for each of the years 1998 - 2000

1998 =

1999 =

Tick the box if statement 3 is correct

2000 =

Question 3

The table shows the percentage of pupils in a school achieving GCSE grades A*- C in English from 1996 to 2000.

Year	1996	1997	1998	1999	2000
Percentage of pupils achieving grades A*- C in English	45	50	42	53	48

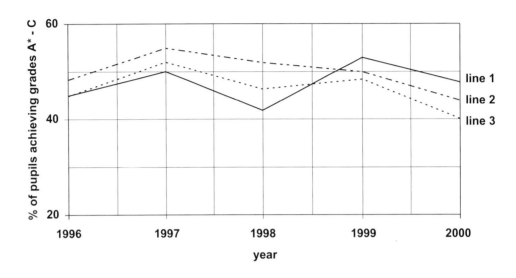

Which line on the graph represents the results for this school?

a. line 1

b. line 2

c. line 3

Question 4

The table shows the number of pupils achieving different Levels in end of Key Stage 2 Mathematics in a school each year from 1998 to 2000.

	Number of pupils achieving different Levels in end of Key Stage 2 Mathematics						
Year	Level 1	Level 2	Level 3	Level 4	Level 5	Level 6	Total
1998	20	29	15	26	10	0	100
1999	6	30	24	35	24	1	120
2000	2	8	34	46	39	1	130

In which Level has there been a ten point increase each year in the percentage of pupils achieving that Level?

a. Level 3

b. Level 4

c. Level 5

Question 5

In a staff meeting about pupil recruitment, the head teacher handed out the following graph showing the number of reception class pupils at three local Primary schools.

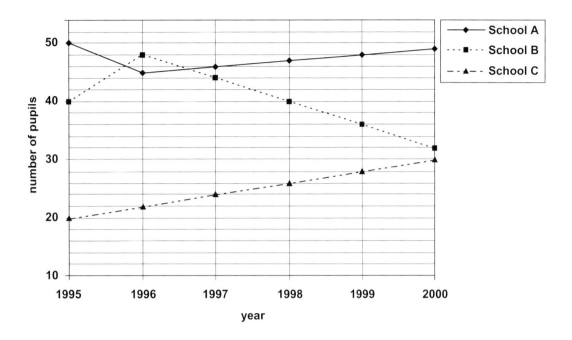

Indicate all the true statements:

1. if trends continue, School A will have 58 pupils in its reception classes in 2002

2. if trends continue, School C will have 20 less reception class pupils than school A in 2001

3. if trends continue, School C will have more pupils in its reception classes than school B in 2001

Question 6

A class teacher is concerned about the attendance of four pupils. The class register for these four pupils for four weeks is shown below.

Pupil	Week 1					Week 2					Week 3					Week 4				
	M	T	W	T	F	M	T	W	T	F	M	T	W	T	F	M	T	W	T	F
A	0	\	/	\	/	0	\	/	\	0	0	\	/	\	0	0	\	/	0	0
B	/	\	/	\	0	/	\	/	\	0	/	\	/	\	0	/	\	/	\	0
C	/	0	/	\	0	/	0	/	\	0	0	/	\	\	0	0	/	\	\	0
D	0	0	/	\	0	0	/	\	0	0	/	\	/	\	0	/	\	/	0	0

/ present am   \ present pm   0 absent

Indicate all the true statements.

1. pupil C has the same attendance record each week

2. the attendance of pupil D improves each week from week 1 to week 4

3. the attendance of pupil A decreases by 10 % each week

Question 7

At a staff meeting, the head teacher gave out the following bar chart showing the percentage of pupils achieving different Levels in end of Key Stage 2 English from 1997 to 2000.

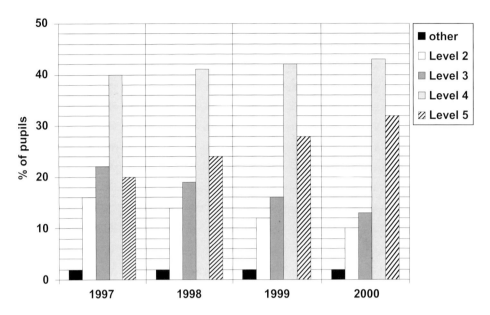

Indicate all the true statements:

1. there has been an increase in the percentage of pupils achieving Level 4 and above each year

2. if the present trend continues, 36% of pupils will achieve Level 5 in 2001

3. the percentage of pupils achieving at Level 2 has fallen each year from 1997 to 2000

Question 8

At the end of a term, a teacher examined a series of test marks out of 50 for three pupils who had been identified as causing concern at the start of the term. These are shown in table 1.

Table 1

Pupil	Test 1	Test 2	Test 3	Test 4	Test 5	Test 6	Test 7	Test 8	Test 9
A	14	14	14	14	14	14	14	14	
B	9	12	15	18	21	24	27	30	
C	5	13	20	26	31	35	38	40	

Table 2

Pupil	X	Y	Z
A	14	14	14
B	33	32	33
C	42	40	41

Circle the letter of the column (**X**, **Y** or **Z**) in table 2 that correctly shows the expected results for Test 9 if the trends shown in Tests 1 - 8 continue.

Section 2 Make comparisons and draw Conclusions

Step by Step Question 1

In a staff meeting at a school, the pupils' percentage marks in a Year 4 benchmarking test were compared with figures for the whole LEA. The Head provided the following Box and Whisker diagrams.

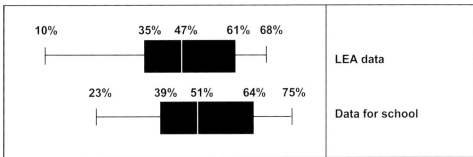

Indicate all the true statements:

1. the difference between the median values was 4 %

2. the inter-quartile range was the same in the school and in the LEA

3. the range for the school was 52 %

Step by step calculation

In this question you are required to use the data in the box and whisker diagrams to find the median, the inter-quartile range and the range of marks. Use the boxes next to each step to write your answers.

To find the difference in the median values

Step 1 Read the median value from the box and whisker diagram of the LEA data.

Step 2 Read the median value from the box and whisker diagram of the school data.

Step 3 Subtract the LEA value from the school value.

Tick the box if statement 1 is correct

To find the inter-quartile range

Step 1 Find the inter-quartile range from the box and whisker diagram of the LEA data by subtracting the lower quartile value from the upper quartile value. (the inter-quartile ranges are shown by the shaded area in the box and whisker diagram).

Step 2 Find the inter-quartile range from the box and whisker diagram of the school data by subtracting the lower quartile value from the upper quartile value.

Tick the box if statement 2 is correct

To find the range for the school

Step 1 Subtract the lower value from the upper value on the box and whisker diagram for the school.

Tick the box if statement 3 is correct

Step by Step Question 2

A head of department gave out a scatter graph showing the GCSE and A level points score of each pupil in a subject.

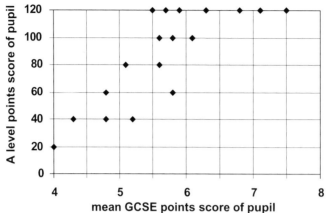

Indicate all the true statements:

1. 10 pupils gained 100 or more A level points and a mean GCSE points score of at least 5.5

2. 4 pupils gained a mean GCSE points score below 5 and scored 40 or less A level points

3. 1/3 of the pupils had a mean GCSE points score of less than 5.5 points.

Step-by-step calculation

This question requires you to read figures from a graph with a two-way axis. You also need to use fractions. Use the boxes next to each step to write your answers.

To work out how many pupils gained 100 or more A level points and a mean GCSE points score of at least 5.5

Step 1 Read up the line at the 5.5 mean GCSE points on the horizontal (x) axis to the 100 A level points line. How many of pupils are to the right of the 5.5 GCSE points line and on or above the 100 A level points line?

Tick the box if statement 1 is true

To work out how many pupils gained a mean GCSE points score of below 5 and also scored 40 or less A level points

Step 1 Read up the line at the 5 mean GCSE points on the horizontal (x) axis to 40 A level points line. How many of the pupils are to the left of the the 5 GCSE points line and on or below the 40 A level points line?

Tick the box if statement 2 is true

To work out if 1/3 of the pupils have a mean GCSE points score of less than 5.5

Step 1 Read up the line at the 5.5 mean GCSE points on horizontal (x) axis and count the number of pupils to the left of this line i.e. the pupils with a mean GCSE point score of less than 5.5

Step 2 Count the total number of pupils on the graph

Step 3 Work out the fraction by dividing the number of pupils with a mean GCSE point score of less than 5.5 by the total number of pupils.

Tick the box if statement 3 is true

Question 3

The cumulative frequency graph shows the percentage of pupils, nationally and in a school, achieving A level grades in Modern Foreign Languages.

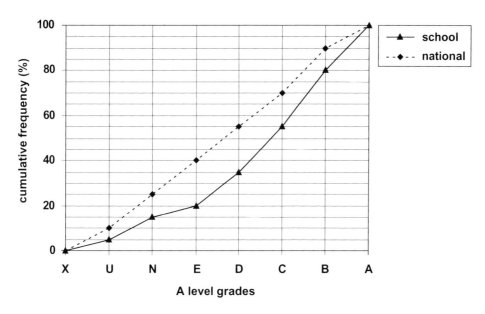

Indicate all the true statements:

1. 20 % less pupils in the school than nationally gained a grade E or lower

2. 20 % more pupils in the school than nationally gained a grade C or better

3. 15 % more pupils in the school than nationally gained a grade C

Question 4

Three classes each sat the same History test marked out of 60.
The table shows the number of pupils in each class achieving a range of marks.

Mark range	Number of pupils achieving each mark range		
	Class A	Class B	Class C
0 - 10	2	6	2
11 - 20	3	7	6
21 - 30	7	5	4
31 - 40	12	6	9
41 - 50	4	4	5
51 - 60	2	2	4
Total	30	30	30

Indicate all the true statements

1. 60 % of class A scored more than half marks

2. the same proportion of pupils in classes A and C scored between 11 and 30 marks

3. 30 % of all pupils scored between 31 and 40 marks

Question 5

The bar chart shows the proportion of pupils in a school achieving Level 5 and above in end of Key Stage 3 tests in English, Mathematics and Science. 150 pupils took the tests in each subject.

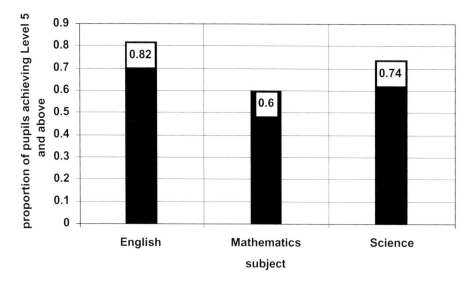

Indicate all the true statements:

1. 90 pupils achieved Level 5 and above in Mathematics

2. 49 pupils achieved less than Level 5 in Science

3. 12 more pupils achieved Level 5 and above in English than did in Science

---

Question 6

The table shows the actual age and the reading age of a group of Year 7 pupils in September 1999 and September 2000.

	September 1999				September 2000			
	Actual age		Reading age		Actual age		Reading age	
Pupil	Years	Months	Years	Months	Years	Months	Years	Months
A	11	2	10	7	12	2	11	7
B	11	0	12	2	12	0	12	11
C	11	7	11	3	12	7	12	9
D	11	3	11	11	12	3	13	6
E	11	9	10	11	12	8	12	0
F	11	1	12	3	12	1	13	7
G	11	7	11	8	12	7	12	3
H	11	6	12	11	12	6	13	10
I	11	4	12	0	12	4	13	6
J	11	5	11	1	12	5	12	10

Indicate all the true statements:

1. the difference in the actual age and reading age of pupil A was the same in 1999 and 2000

2. in September 2000, 2 pupils had a difference between their actual age and their reading age of 4 months or less

3. pupil J made the greatest improvement between September 1999 and September 2000

Question 7

The option choices of pupils in three different classes in Year 9 are shown in the table.

	Option choice			
	Geography	German	History	Drama
Class A	10	4	3	11
Class B	6	5	10	9
Class C	8	4	7	8
Total number of pupils	24	13	20	28

Circle the subject where 65 % of the total number of pupils choosing the subject came from classes A and B.

Question 8

To put together a Year 6 class worksheet on fitness, a teacher collected some data from three pupils. This is shown in the table below.

Pupil	Height / m	Weight / kg
A	1.20	53
B	1.30	29
C	1.42	49

The diagram shown below allows pupils in the class to estimate their percentage fat from their height and weight. The teacher plotted lines on the diagram for each of pupils A, B and C to show the class how to estimate the percentage of fat.

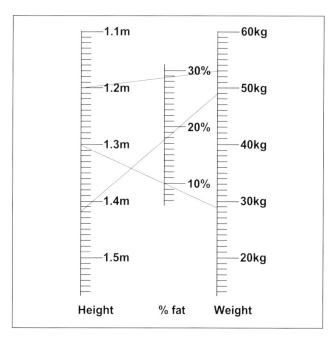

Indicate all the true statements:

1. the difference between the estimated percentage fat of pupils A and B is more than 17 %
2. pupil B has a lower estimated percentage fat than pupil C
3. pupil A has a higher estimated percentage fat than pupil B, but not pupil C

Section 3 Interpretation of Data

Step by Step Question 1

The table shows the cumulative frequency of GCSE Science results for a school in 2000.

	GCSE Science grades
Grade	Cumulative frequency
A*	7
A	19
B	47
C	93
D	121
E	142
F	158
G	175
U	186

Indicate all the true statements:

☐ 1. 175 pupils achieved a grade G

☐ 2. the same number of pupils achieved a grade B and grade D

☐ 3. 50 % of pupils achieved grades A* - C

Step-by-step calculation

This question requires you to use cumulative frequency numbers to work out percentages and actual numbers. Cumulative frequency adds each category to the previous total, giving the final total at the end. Use the boxes next to each step to write your answers.

To work out number of pupils who achieved grade G

Step 1 Calculate the number of pupils achieving grade G by subtracting the cumulative frequency at grade F from the cumulative frequency at grade G

Tick the box if statement 1 is correct

To work out the number of pupils who achieved grade B and grade D

Step 1 Calculate the number of pupils achieving grade B by subtracting the cumulative frequency at grade A from the cumulative frequency at grade B

Step 2 Calculate the number of pupils achieving grade D by subtracting the cumulative frequency at grade C from the cumulative frequency at grade D

Tick the box if statement 2 is correct

To work out the percentage of pupils who achieved grades A*-C

Step 1 Read off, from the table, the cumulative number of pupils who achieved grade A*-C (this is the value at row C)

Step 2 Read off the total number of pupils from the table (this is the last number in the cumulative frequency column)

Step 3 Convert the number in step 1 to a percentage. Use the formula:
Percentage of pupils A*-C = (number ÷ total number of pupils) x 100

Tick the box if statement 3 is true

Step by Step Question 2

A teacher made estimates of pupil's GCSE grades based on their mock examination results.
The table shows the estimates.

Mock examination mark (%)	less than 35	35 - 44	45 - 54	55 - 64	65 - 74	75 - 84	85 +
Estimated GCSE grade	G	F	E	D	C	B	A or A*

The scatter graph shows the mock examination mark for 7 pupils and their actual GCSE grade.

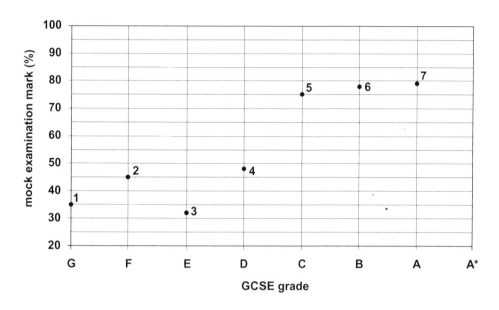

Circle the number of the pupil who gained a GCSE grade two grades better than their estimated grade.

Step by step calculation

In this question you are expected to look for a relationship between the performance of an individual pupil in two different examinations by matching two sets of data. Use the boxes next to each step to write your answers.

To compare the actual grade for pupil 1 with the mock examination estimated grade

Step 1 Read along the horizontal (x) axis to find the GCSE grade for pupil 1

Step 2 Read along the vertical (y) axis to find the mock examination mark for pupil 1

Step 3 Find the estimated grade from the mock examination mark from the table

Step 4 Compare the estimated grade to the actual grade

Repeat steps 1 – 4 for all the pupils and complete the table below

Pupil	2	3	4	5	6	7
GCSE grade						
Mock examination mark						
Estimated GCSE grade						

Circle the number of the correct pupil on the graph

Question 3

The bar chart shows the end of Key Stage 3 Science results in a school for 1999 and 2000.
180 pupils took the tests in 1999 and 210 pupils took the tests in 2000.

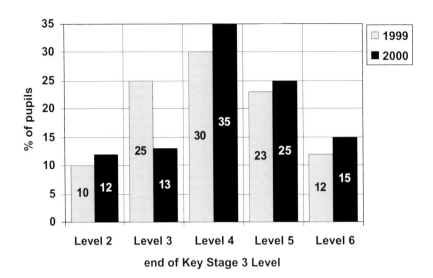

Indicate all the true statements:

1. the same number of pupils achieved at Level 4 in both years

2. in both years less than 24 pupils achieved at Level 2

3. the number of pupils achieving Level 5 and above rose by 21 between 1999 and 2000

Question 4

The table shows the percentage of pupils achieving different Levels in end of Key Stage 2 Science from 1996 to 2000.

(B = boys, G = girls)

	Percentage of pupils achieving different Levels in end of Key Stage 2 Science											
	Working to Level 1		Level 1		Level 2		Level 3		Level 4		Level 5	
Year	B	G	B	G	B	G	B	G	B	G	B	G
2000	0	0	1	0	3	2	17	17	51	53	27	27
1999	0	0	1	0	4	3	20	20	51	54	24	22
1998	0	0	1	0	4	3	24	23	51	55	19	17
1997	0	0	1	0	5	4	25	25	50	53	19	17
1996	0	0	1	1	6	5	29	27	48	52	16	15

(figures may not add up to 100 due to rounding)

Indicate all the true statements:

1. the percentage of boys achieving Level 4 and above increased each year from 1996 to 2000

2. the difference in the percentage of boys and girls achieving Level 4 and above in 1996 was 5 %

3. the percentage of girls achieving at Level 3 increased by 2 percentage points each year

Question 5

The graph shows the total number of pupils admitted to Year 7 of a Secondary school and the numbers admitted from two feeder Primary schools, A and B, each year from 1996 to 2000.

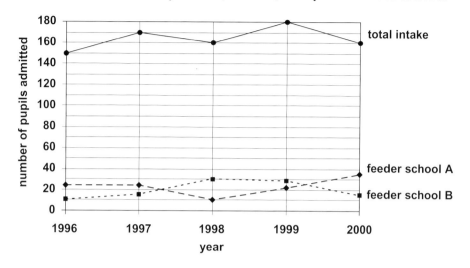

In which year did the total number of pupils admitted from feeder schools A and B represent 25 % of the total intake?

	a. 1996
	b. 1998
	c. 1999

Question 6

A primary school head teacher presented the following cumulative frequency bar chart at a staff meeting.

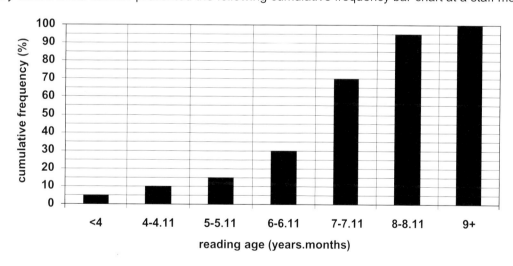

Indicate all the true statements:

	1. 55% of pupils had a reading age between 6 years and 7 years 11 months
	2. 90% of pupils had a reading age of 4 years and above
	3. there were more pupils in the range 7-7.11 than in any other age range

Question 7

A teacher surveyed the absences in Years 7, 8 and 9 over a six-week period. The percentage of pupils absent on a Friday afternoon of each week was recorded. The table shows the number of pupils in each year group and the graph shows the results of the absence survey.

Year group	Year 7	Year 8	Year 9
Number of pupils	175	180	180

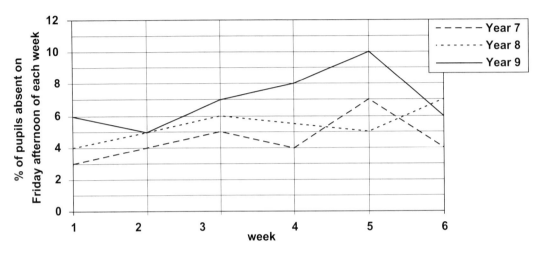

Indicate all the true statements:

1. 9 pupils from Year 8 were absent on Friday afternoon of week 5

2. a total of 25 pupils from Years 7, 8 and 9 were absent on Friday afternoon of week 2

3. absences in all three year groups was higher in week 5 than in week 4

Question 8

The table shows the number of pupils in each Year group of an 11-16 school in June 2000.

Year group	Year 7	Year 8	Year 9	Year 10	Year 11
Number of pupils	195	218	212	223	205

In July 2000, all Year 11 pupils leave the school.
The following changes take place in September 2000.

> All pupils move up a year
> 227 pupils enter Year 7
> 9 pupils from Year 9 move to other schools
> 5 pupils join Year 10

How many pupils will be on roll in September 2000?

Using and Applying general Arithmetic

Section 4 Time

Step by Step Question 1

Part of a teacher's plan for a lesson of 70 minutes is shown below.

Lesson outline – storyboarding	
Activity	Time in minutes
Teacher introduction	5
Teacher reads start of a story	5
Pupil groups do a storyboard after the reading	10
Teacher explains how to complete the story	5
Whole class discussion to brainstorm ideas	5
Pupil groups divide up drawing tasks	10
Pupil groups complete storyboards	10
Individual pupils draw pictures	15
Teacher concludes lesson	5

Circle the letter of the pie chart that correctly shows the proportion of the lesson spent in each of the different types of activity.

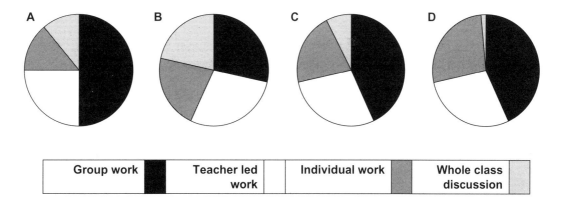

Step-by-step calculation

In this question you are required to look for patterns in a pie chart consistent or inconsistent with the data in the table. Use the boxes next to each step to write your answers.

To calculate the amount of time spent in each type of activity

Step 1 Add the total time spent in each different activity

Group work

Teacher led work

Individual work

Whole class discussion

	minutes
	minutes
	minutes
	minutes

Step 2 Look at each of the pie charts and match the data to the pattern from Step 1

Pie chart A. Is group work half of the 70 minutes?

Pie chart B. Should the smaller sectors be the same size?

Pie chart C. Do all the categories have different values?

Pie chart D. Should the smallest sector be so small?

You should have eliminated 3 pie charts, and therefore the remaining one is correct

Circle the letter of the correct pie chart

Step by Step Question 2

A school term is 15 weeks long including half term.
Half term is one week half way through the term.
Lessons in the school are 80 minutes long.
A class has 2 lessons per week in a curriculum area.

How much teaching time will have been spent on this curriculum area by half term?
Give your answer in hours and minutes.

Step-by-step calculation

This question requires you to convert a number of lessons to the total time spent in lessons.
It can be answered by following various sequences of operations. Work through the suggested sequence.
Use the boxes next to each step to write your answers.

Step 1 Calculate the number of weeks to half term

Step 2 Calculate the number of lessons to half term by multiplying the
number of weeks by the number of lessons per week

Step 3 Calculate the number of minutes to half term by multiplying the
number of lessons to half term by the length of a lesson in minutes

Step 4 Calculate the number of hours by dividing by 60 to give a whole
number of hours and a remainder

Step 5 Multiply the remainder by 60 to give the number of minutes

Write your answer in the space provided after the question

Question 3

A teacher planned a walk for a group of pupils.
The diagram shows the proposed plan.

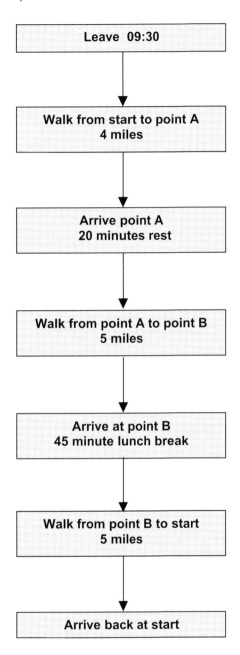

The pupils walked at a mean speed of 3.5 miles per hour.
At what time did they arrive back at the starting point?
Give your answer using the 24-hour clock.

Question 4

A school day starts at 08:50 and ends at 15:25.
Morning break is 15 minutes and lunch break is 1 hour.
The school day has 8 lessons each of equal length.
A teacher teaches 7 lessons on a Tuesday.
How much time is spent teaching on a Tuesday?
Give your answer in hours and minutes.

```
┌─────────────────┐
│                 │
│                 │
└─────────────────┘
```

Question 5

A school has 8 periods in a day, each lasting 40 minutes.
The diagram shows the periods when the library is available to Year 13 pupils for private study.

Day	Period 1	2	3	4	5	Lunch	6	7	8
Monday	■	■		▨	▨				■
Tuesday		▨		■	■		▨	▨	▨
Wednesday	■	▨	■	▨				■	■
Thursday	▨			■	■		▨		
Friday	■	■	▨	▨	▨			▨	▨

■ used by Years 7, 8 and 9.   ▨ used by Years 10, 11 and 12.

☐ available to Year 13.

In addition, the library is available to Year 13 for 1/2 hour each lunch time on Monday, Wednesday and Friday.
For how long is the library available to Year 13 each week?
Give your answer in hours and minutes.

```
┌─────────────────┐
│                 │
│                 │
└─────────────────┘
```

Question 6

A school provides a report twice a year for each of its pupils.

A teacher teaches 30 Year 7 pupils, 59 Year 8 pupils, 56 Year 9 pupils and 60 Year 10 pupils.
Each report takes 5 minutes to write.
How much time is spent writing reports during the year?
Give your answer in hours and minutes.

```
┌─────────────────┐
│                 │
│                 │
└─────────────────┘
```

Question 7

The table shows the homework timetable for Year 9 in a Secondary school.
The recommended time to be spent per homework session is 30 minutes on each of English, Mathematics and Science and 20 minutes on each other subject.

Day	Homework subject		
Monday	Science	History	English
Tuesday	Geography	Mathematics	English
Wednesday	Religious education	Mathematics	Drama
Thursday	Information Technology	Design and Technology	Mathematics
Friday	Design and Technology	Information Technology	Science

Indicate all the true statements:

1. the homework timetable sets a total of 3 hours 30 minutes per week for English, Mathematics and Science

2. the time set for History and Geography homework is 1 hour and 20 minutes per week

3. the time set for homework is 1 hour and 20 minutes each day

Question 8

A teacher planned a visit to a farm, leaving school at 09:00.
The table shows the proposed plan for the visit.

Activity	Proposed timing
Travel to the farm	45 minutes
Introduction and tour	1 hour 30 minutes
Feeding the lambs	50 minutes
Cleaning up	15 minutes
Lunch	1 hour
Pond dipping project	1 hour 15 minutes
Milking shed visit	1 hour
Travel back to school	45 minutes

At what time should the teacher expect to return to school at the end of the day?
Give your answer using the 24-hour clock.

Section 5 Money

Step by Step Question 1

A school department has a budget of £1875.
£684 is spent on a new computer, £488 on new equipment, £223 on consumables and £227 on printing and photocopying.
The remaining money is used to purchase textbooks costing £7.99 each.

Indicate all the true statements:

1. 24 % of the budget is spent on consumables, printing and photocopying

2. 25 % of the budget is spent on new equipment

3. 31 textbooks are purchased

Step-by-step calculation

This question requires you to calculate percentages using information about expenditure on individual items. You will also need to add, subtract and divide using money. Use the boxes next to each step to write your answers.

To find the percentage of the budget spent on consumables, printing and photocopying

Step 1 Add up the total money spent on consumables (£223), printing and photocopying (£227)

£

Step 2 Calculate the percentage of the total budget using the total from step 1.
Use the formula: Percentage = (expenditure ÷ total budget) x100

£

Tick the box if statement 1 is true

To find the percentage of the budget spent on new equipment

Step 1 Calculate the percentage of the total budget using the data in the question.
Use the formula: Percentage = (expenditure ÷ total budget) x100

£

Tick the box if the statement 2 is true

To find the number of text books purchased

Step 1 Calculate the amount of money available for textbooks by adding the total money spent and subtracting it from the total budget

£

Step 2 Calculate the number of text books by dividing the total from step 1 by the cost of the textbooks

Tick the box if statement 3 is true

Step by Step Question 2

A teacher went on an in-service training course.
The table shows the mileage recorded before and after the trip.

Mileage before	96415
Mileage after	96538

The teacher can claim 33p per mile for the first 100 miles, and then 22p per mile for any distance above 100 miles.

How much should the teacher claim for travelling expenses?

Step by step calculation

In this question you are expected to work out a distance travelled in miles and carry out a two stage calculation using pounds and pence. It can be answered by following various sequences of operations, but all contain the same basic steps. Work through the suggested sequence of steps. Use the boxes next to each step to write your answers.

To calculate the distance travelled

Step 1   Subtract the starting mileage from the final mileage

miles

Step 2   Calculate the distance in excess of 100 miles. Use the formula:
Distance = Actual distance (from step 1) – 100

miles

To calculate the mileage costs

Step 1   Calculate the cost per mile in pounds (£) for the first 100 miles
by dividing 33 by 100

£

Step 2   Calculate the cost per mile in pounds (£) for miles above 100 miles
by dividing 22 by 100

£

Step 3   Calculate the claim for the first 100 miles using the formula:
Claim = cost per mile (from step 1) x 100

£

Step 4   Calculate the claim for the remaining miles using the formula:
Claim = cost per mile (from step 2) x distance (from step 2
in the previous calculation)

£

Step 5   Calculate the overall claim by adding the claim from step 3 and
the claim from step 4

£

Write your answer in the space provided at the end of the question

Question 3

The table shows the amount of printing done by members of a department during one term.

Member of staff	Photocopying (Black and white at 3p per copy)	Photocopying (Colour at 6p per copy)	Printing (Black and white at 1.5p per copy)
A	475	65	280
B	450	68	320
C	540	45	240
D	595	20	450
E	395	108	330

Circle the letters of the two members of staff who spent most on photocopying.

Question 4

A school has 1380 pupils and 64 staff.
As part of a fund raising event, the school had a non-uniform day.
Each pupil paid 60 pence and each member of staff paid £2.50.
The money raised was divided equally between 4 charities.
How much money did each charity receive?

Question 5

In 2000, a department had a budget of £1500.
In that year, the department was over spent by £165.
In 2001, the department was given the same budget as 1999 plus an 8 % increase.
The over spend was then deducted from the new budget.
How much did the department receive in 2001?

Question 6

A teacher was planning a pond for the nature area of a school.
The size of pond liner needed was 9 metres by 7 metres.

Which would be the cheapest way of buying the liner?

☐ a. off a roll 9 metres wide, cost £31 per metre length of the liner

☐ b. at a cost of £3.48 per square metre

☐ c. off a roll 8 metres wide, cost £30 per metre length of the liner

---

Question 7

As part of a fund raising day for charity, a class of 30 pupils ran sponsored laps of the school playing fields.
Each pupil was sponsored at the rate of 75p per lap.
The table shows the number of pupils and the laps they completed.

Number of laps completed	10	12	14	16	18	20
Number of pupils	3	2	7	9	6	3

The money raised was divided equally between 3 charities.
How much did each charity receive?

☐

Question 8

A Modern Foreign Languages department ordered new sets of textbooks.
The table shows the number of books ordered and the cost.

Book	Number of books ordered	Cost per book	Discount	Minimum order for discount
A	30	£5.90	5 %	30 books
B	25	£7.99	5 %	£200
C	30	£4.95	None	not applicable
D	50	£3.50	10 %	£150

What was the total cost of the order after any discounts?

☐

52

Section 6 Proportions and Ratio

Step by Step Question 1

The table shows the distance travelled to school by Primary school pupils and the method of transport.

Distance travelled	Number of pupils travelling to school by			
	Car	Bus	Walking	Cycling
0 to 0.9 miles	11	5	23	10
1.0 to 1.9 miles	16	8	13	5
2.0 to 2.9 miles	(1)	19	0	8
3.0 to 3.9 miles	27	21	0	1
Over 4 miles	31	19	0	0
Total number of pupils	108	72	36	24
Proportion of pupils	0.45	0.3	(2)	0.1

Select and write the correct values in the boxes (1) and (2) to complete the table.

| 21 | 23 | 24 |

| 0.05 | 0.15 | 0.175 |

Step-by-step calculation

This question requires you to calculate a number and a proportion as a decimal. Use the boxes next to each step to write your answers.

To work out the number of pupils travelling between 2-0 to 2-9 miles by car

Step 1 Read from the table, the total number of pupils travelling by car

Step 2 Add up the total number of pupils travelling 0 - 0.9 miles, 1.0 – 1.9 miles, 3.0 – 3.9 miles and more than 4 miles

Step 3 Subtract the total (from step 2) from the total (from step 1)

Select the correct value from the numbers in the boxes and write it in box 1 in the table

To work out the proportion of pupils walking to school

Step 1 Add together the numbers in the row 'Total of Number of Pupils' This will give the total of all pupils

Step 2 Divide the total number of pupils walking to school by the total from Step 1 to get the proportion

Select the correct value from the numbers in the boxes and write it in box 2 in the table

Step by Step Question 2

The bar chart shows the number of boys and girls in each of 6 classes in a Year group.

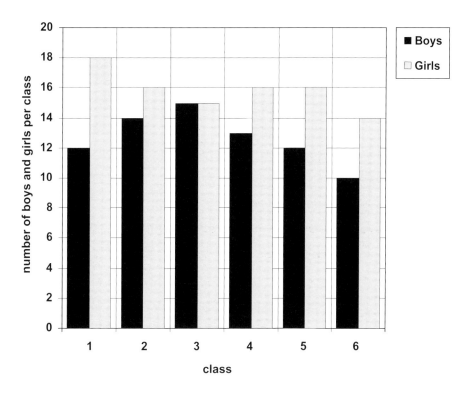

What is the ratio of boys to girls in the Year group? Give your answer in its simplest form.

Step by step calculation

In this question you are required to read information from the bar chart and use it to obtain a ratio. This also requires division of numbers to reach the simplest form. Use the boxes next to each step to write your answers.

To find the ratio of boys to girls in the Year group

Step 1 Add the number of boys in each class to find the total number of boys

Step 2 Add the number of girls in each class to find the total number of girls

Step 3 Write the two numbers next to each other (boys first) and cancel to a simpler form. If you cannot find a common denominator straight away, keep dividing by the same number until the simplest form is reached

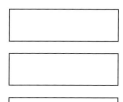

Write your answer in the box at the end of the question

Question 3

The bar chart shows the number of pupils in a Primary school achieving different Levels in end of Key Stage 1 English.

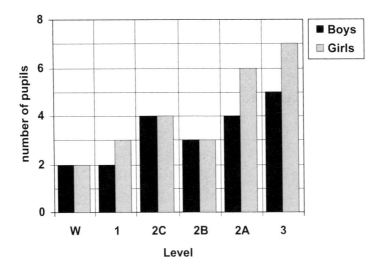

What is the ratio of girls to boys who achieved Level 2B and above?

Question 4

The table shows the numbers of pupils in 9 classes achieving different grades in GCSE English.

	Number of pupils in each class achieving grade									
Class	A*	A	B	C	D	E	F	G	U	Total pupils
1	1	2	7	12	6	1	1	0	0	30
2	0	1	5	14	5	2	2	0	1	30
3	0	2	4	12	6	2	3	1	0	30
4	2	3	10	10	2	2	1	0	0	30
5	3	4	12	6	5	0	0	0	0	30
6	0	2	6	9	8	2	1	2	0	30
7	1	4	4	11	7	2	0	1	0	30
8	1	1	4	5	4	6	5	2	2	30
9	0	3	4	7	5	7	1	3	0	30

Indicate all the true statements:

1. the proportion of pupils achieving grades A* - C was the same in classes 2 and 7

2. 1/5 of the pupils in class 5 achieved grade D

3. class 8 had the smallest proportion of pupils who achieved grades A* - G

Question 5

The cumulative frequency table below shows the distance travelled to school by 65 pupils at a small village Primary school.

Distance travelled to school (km)	Cumulative frequency	Proportion
Less than 2	15	
2.1- 4	34	
4.1- 6	44	
6.1- 8	52	
8.1- 10	61	
over 10.1	65	

Circle the letter of the table (**A**, **B** or **C**) below that shows the correct values for the proportion of pupils travelling different distances to school.

A	B	C
0.15	0.00	0.23
0.34	0.23	0.52
0.44	0.52	0.68
0.52	0.68	0.80
0.61	0.80	0.94
0.65	0.94	1.00

Question 6

Teachers in a department looked at the A level achievement of pupils over a three-year period. The A level grades of pupils in the department are given in the table below.

	Number of pupils achieving grade					
Year	Fail	E	D	C	B	A
1998	6	7	7	15	12	11
1999	7	6	11	13	15	12
2000	4	5	13	15	15	14

Circle the correct year in which the ratio of the combined Fail, E, D results to the combined C, B, A results was exactly 1:2

Question 7

A head of department gave out the following pie chart in a discussion document about qualifications on entry to an A level course with 150 pupils.

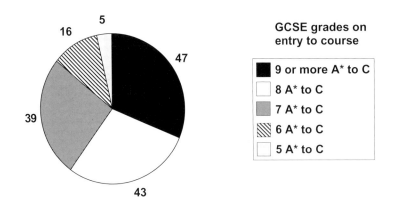

	Proportion		
Number of GCSEs on entry	X	Y	Z
8 or more A* to C grades	0.29	0.60	1.67
7 or less A* to C grades	0.71	0.40	3.75

Circle the letter (**X**, **Y** or **Z**) of the column in the table that shows the correct proportions of GCSE grades on entry to the A level subject in 2001.

Question 8

A school recorded its GCSE examination results for English, Mathematics and Science in 2001.

	Number of pupils achieving each grade in		
GCSE grade	English	Mathematics	Science
A*	5	3	2
A	7	13	6
B	23	23	24
C	37	36	41
D	29	46	31
E	20	13	27
F	14	10	13
G	14	4	9
U	5	8	4
Total	154	156	157

In which subject did the highest proportion of candidates achieve grades A* - C?

☐ a. English

☐ b. Mathematics

☐ c. Science

Section 7 Percentages, Fractions and Decimals

Step by Step Question 1

The pie chart was used by the head of a school at a staff meeting to discuss liaison with education providers for Year 11 leavers.

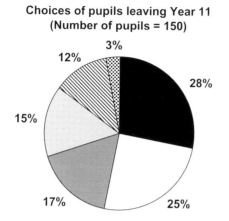

Choices of pupils leaving Year 11
(Number of pupils = 150)

- ■ A level
- ☐ Employment
- ▨ AVCE
- ☐ GNVQ
- ▧ GCSE resits
- ▦ Other

Indicate all the true statements:

1. 1/4 of the pupils intend to enter employment

2. 81 pupils intend to follow an A level course

3. more pupils will do an AVCE course than will do GNVQ

4. 3/4 of the pupils intend to stay in education

Step-by-step calculation

This question requires you to convert percentages to fractions and to whole numbers. As statements 1 and 4 are both fractions it is easier to do these at the same time. Similarly, as statements 2 and 3 are whole numbers these can also be calculated at the same time. Use the boxes next to each step to write your answers.

To find the fraction intending to enter employment

Step 1 Read the percentage from the pie chart

%

Step 2 Convert the percentage to a fraction. Use the formula:
Fraction = answer to step 1 ÷ 100
Reduce the fraction to its simplest form

Tick the box if statement 1 is correct

To find the fraction intending to stay in education

Step 1 Add the percentages of pupils for all education options

| A level = | AVCE = | GNVQ = | GCSE = | Total = |
| % | % | % | % | % |

Step 2 Convert the percentage to a fraction using the formula above

Tick the box if statement 4 is correct

To find the numbers intending to do A level

Step 1   Find the total percentage intending to do A level from the pie chart

Total =   %

Step 2   Calculate the number from the percentage from step 1. Use the formula:
Number = (total in school x total percentage) ÷100

Tick the box if statement 2 is correct

To find out if more pupils will do an AVCE course than will do a GNVQ course

Step 1   Find the percentage intending to AVCE from the pie chart

Total =   %

Step 2   Find the percentage intending to GNVQ from the pie chart

Total =   %

Step 3   Compare the two percentages of the same total number of pupils
The higher percentage is the greater number
There is no need to calculate the actual numbers

Tick the box if statement 3 is correct

Step by Step Question 2

An English department analysed its end of Key Stage 3 results for the year 2001.

Level	2	3	4	5	6	7	8
Number of pupils achieving each Level in end of Key Stage 3 English	5	18	31	26	21	16	3

The department set a target of 5 percentage points for an increase from 2001 to 2002 in the proportion of pupils achieving Level 5 and above. 140 pupils were due to sit the end of Key Stage 3 English tests in year 2002.

What is the minimum number of pupils who would need to achieve Level 5 and above in 2002 if the target is to be met?

Step by step calculation

In this question you are required to work out a percentage increase from the information in the table. Use the boxes next to each step to write your answers.

To find the percentage achieving Level 5 and above in year 2001

Step 1   Add up the number of pupils achieving Level 5 and above using the information in the table

Step 2   Add up the total number of pupils taking end of Key Stage 3 English

Step 3   Find the percentage. Use the formula:
Percentage = [number (from step 1)] ÷ [total number (from step 2)] x 100

To find the minimum number of pupils to improve by five percentage points

Step 1   Add 5 percentage points to the percentage calculated in step 3 of the previous section

Step 2   Convert this to the minimum number of pupils for 2002. Use the formula:
Number = Percentage x total number of pupils for 2002 ÷100

Write your answer in the box at the end of the question

Question 3

The diagram shows a timetable for a newly qualified teacher.
All lessons last for the same length of time.

	Period								
Day	1	2	Break	3	4	Lunch	5	6
Mon	Maths Year 8	Maths Year 8		Non - contact			Maths Year 7	Maths Year 7
Tues.	ICT Year 9	ICT Year 9		Maths Year 8	Maths Year 8		ICT Year 7	ICT Year 7
Wed.	Maths Year 7	Maths Year 7		Non - contact			Maths Year 10	Maths Year 10
Thurs.	ICT Year 8	Maths Year 10		Maths Year 8	Maths Year 8		Maths Year 9	Maths Year 9
Fri.	ICT Year 8	ICT Year 8		Maths Year 9	Maths Year 9		Non - contact	

Indicate all the true statements:

1. 1/5 of total teaching time is spent teaching ICT

2. 25 % of total teaching time is spent teaching Year 7

3. 17 lessons are spent teaching Mathematics

Question 4

Table 1 shows the groups into which the DfES place schools according to the percentage of pupils in the school receiving Free School Meals.

Table 1

School group	% of pupils receiving Free School Meals
1	up to 5 %
2	5.1 to 9 %
3	9.1 to 13 %
4	13.1 to 21 %
5	21.1 to 35 %
6	35.1 to 50 %
7	more than 50 %

Table 2 shows the total number of pupils in each Year group in a Secondary school and the number of pupils in each Year group receiving Free School Meals.

Table 2

	Year 7	Year 8	Year 9	Year 10	Year 11
Total number of pupils in each Year group	168	159	180	162	165
Number of pupils receiving Free school meals	33	41	36	39	28

To which group does the school belong?

Question 5

A GCSE subject has two components:

component A - coursework worth 25%
component B - final examination worth 75%.

A mark of 60% overall is needed for a grade C.

A candidate scores 50 out of 63 for coursework.
The final examination is marked out of 110 marks.
What is the minimum mark the candidate needs to score on the final examination to gain a grade C?

Question 6

At a staff meeting, a head teacher presented the following cumulative frequency graph for a Year group of 75 pupils.

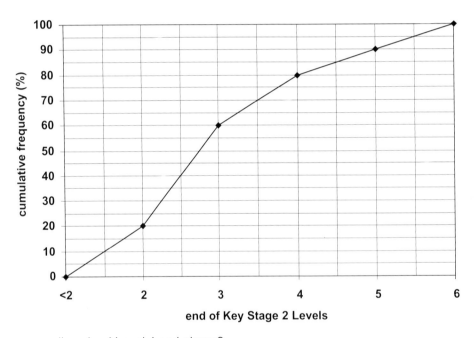

How many pupils gained Level 4 and above?

a. 15

b. 30

c. 40

Question 7

The table shows the absences for 6 classes in a Year group during the Spring term.

Class	Number of pupils	Absences during Spring term			
		Maximum number of 1/2 day attendances	Total number of authorised absences	Total number of unauthorised absences	Absence rate as percentage
A	(28 pupils)	3360	157	75	6.90 %
B	(30 pupils)	3600	100	78	4.94 %
C	(30 pupils)	3600	149	89	6.61 %
D	(29 pupils)	3480	185	98	8.13 %
E	(28 pupils)	3360	(1)	119	6.31 %
F	(27 pupils)	3240	117	68	(2)

Select and write the correct values in the boxes **(1)** and **(2)** to complete the table.

92	93	94
5.70 %	5.71 %	5.80 %

Question 8

A GCSE subject has two coursework components:

Component 1 is worth 40 % of the overall coursework marks.
Component 2 is worth 60 % of the overall coursework marks.

A pupil scored 45 out of 60 in component 1 and 56 out of 80 in component 2.
What was the pupil's overall percentage mark for coursework?

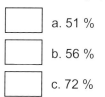

a. 51 %

b. 56 %

c. 72 %

Section 8 Measurements

Step by Step Question 1

The diagram shows a plan of a school Science laboratory.

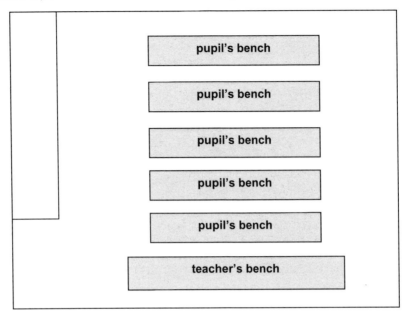

The pupil's benches measure 4.5 m by 1.1 m.
As part of a refurbishment, the pupil's benches are to be removed and replaced with 5 square benches, each measuring 2.5 m by 2.5 m.
How much additional bench space will be available?
Give your answer in square metres.

Step by step calculation

This question requires you to work out areas in metres (m) using arithmetical processes. Make sure in questions using measurement that you give the units. Use the boxes next to each step to write your answers.

To work out the area of the existing pupil benches

Step 1 Calculate the area of one bench. Use the formula:
Area = length x width

> Area =
> Square metres

Step 2 Calculate the total bench area by multiplying the area from step 1 by the number of benches

> Total area =
> Square metres

To work out the additional area available

Step 1 Calculate the area of one replacement bench. Use the formula:
Area = length x width

> Area =
> Square metres

Step 2 Calculate the total bench area by multiplying the area from step 1 by the number of benches

> Total area =
> Square metres

Step 3 Subtract the total from step 2 of the previous calculation from the total of step 2 in this calculation

> Difference =
> Square metres

Write your answer in the box at the end of the question

Step by Step Question 2

A teacher was planning a pond for the nature area of a school. In a book, the teacher found a formula for calculating how much pond liner to use.

Length of liner (in metres) = (maximum length of pond + maximum depth of pond) x 1.8
Width of liner (in metres) = (maximum width of pond + maximum depth of pond) x 1.8

The diagram shows the proposed pond. Each square is 0.5 m x 0.5 m

Maximum depth 0.9m

width

length

Indicate all the true statements:

1. the pond will be 2.5 metres wide

2. the pond liner will be 5.22 m wide

3. the pond liner will be 9.72 m long

Step by step calculation

In this question you are required to use information from a diagram to work out areas and distance in metres. Use the boxes next to each step to write your answers.

To find the width of the pond

Step 1 Count the number of squares across the maximum width of the pond map on the diagram

Step 2 Convert the value from step 1 to a distance by multiplying by 0.5m

Tick the box if statement 1 is correct

To find the width of the pond liner

Step 1 Count the number of squares across the maximum width of the pond map on the diagram

Step 2 Convert the value from step 1 to a distance by multiplying by 0.5m

Step 3 Use the formula given in the question to convert to a width of pond liner

Tick the box if statement 2 is correct

To find the length of the pond liner

Step 1 Count the number of squares across the maximum length of the pond map on the diagram.

Step 2 Covert the value from step 1 to a distance by multiplying by 0.5m

Step 3 Use the formula given in the question to convert to a length of pond liner

Tick the box if statement 3 is correct

Question 3

A teacher prepared a numeracy lesson in which a group of pupils would measure the length of three windowsills using 15 cm rulers laid end to end. Two windowsills are 1.65m long and one windowsill is 2.55m long.

How many rulers would be needed to lay out end to end along all three windowsills simultaneously?

a. 38

b. 39

c. 40

Question 4

A Primary school classroom has 3 display boards each measuring 1.75 m by 1.0 m.

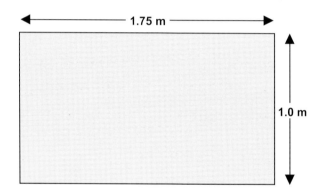

Pupils have produced work for display on pieces of card measuring 180 mm by 260 mm. These pieces of work are to be displayed portrait style as shown.

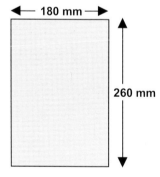

What is the maximum number of pieces of work that can be displayed on the 3 boards without overlap?

Question 5

A teacher was planning a display board for Year 2 pupils' work. The teacher had some 2 cm wide ribbon and wanted to find out if there was enough to put on the board around the edge.

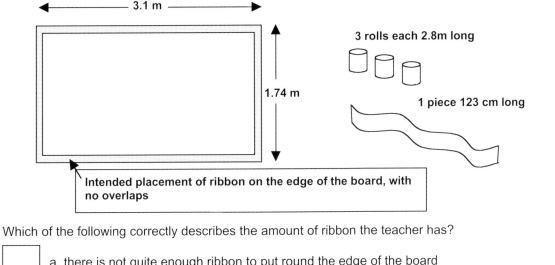

3 rolls each 2.8m long

1 piece 123 cm long

Intended placement of ribbon on the edge of the board, with no overlaps

Which of the following correctly describes the amount of ribbon the teacher has?

a. there is not quite enough ribbon to put round the edge of the board

b. there is exactly enough ribbon to put round the edge of the board

c. there will be a bit of ribbon left after it has been put round the edge of the board

Question 6

A teacher compared the price of cork tiles for a class project.
The area to be covered was 2 m x 1.25 m.
The teacher's diary said "to convert square feet to square metres, multiply by 0.0929".

Supplier	Price per pack	Area covered per pack
A	£5.99	2.5 m^2
B	£2.99	2.0 m^2
C	£5.50	30 square feet

Which supplier would able to supply sufficient cork tiles for the lowest price?

Question 7

A teacher planned for a class of 30 pupils each to set up a 1 litre brine shrimp culture as part of a KS1 project. Each pupil would need to measure out 35 g of sea salt for their culture, and count out 100 brine shrimp eggs to get it started.

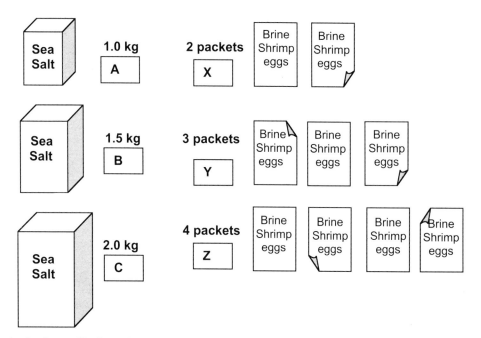

Circle the letter (**A**, **B** or **C**) of the smallest size pack of sea salt that would be big enough for the class, and circle the number of packs (**X**, **Y** or **Z**) of 800 brine shrimp eggs required for the class.

Question 8

A group of pupils submitted a Duke of Edinburgh Expedition plan including the following information:

> **Leave camp at 09:00**
>
> **Distance to be walked before lunch = 15 kilometres**
>
> **Lunch = 1 hour**
>
> **Distance to be walked after lunch = 13.5 kilometres**
>
> **Arrive at new campsite at 17:00**

What is the correct average speed in kilometres per hour at which the pupils must walk both before and after lunch to achieve the target they have set?

- [ ] a. 0.3
- [ ] b. 3.6
- [ ] c. 4.1

Section 9 Conversions

Step by Step Question 1

The table shows the amount of money brought back from a school trip to Germany by a group of pupils.

Pupil	Deutsche marks (DM)
A	25
B	36
C	27
D	18
E	12
F	31

On return to England, the teacher in charge of the trip collected the money and exchanged it into pounds sterling at the exchange rate of £1 = 3.06 DM.
How much money did the teacher receive after paying a 5 % commission?
Give your answer in pounds and pence.

Step by step calculation

This question requires you to convert a sum of money in Deutsche Marks (DM) into pounds sterling. The exchange rate you are asked to work with is an approximation as the actual values vary depending on the currency markets. Use the boxes next to each step to write your answers.

To work out the total collected

Step 1 Add the amounts in DM returned by each pupil

Total =   DM

Step 2 Divide the total in DM by the exchange rate to find the sterling value

£

To work out the amount received by the teacher

Step 1 Calculate the commission by finding 5 % of the sterling value.
Use the formula: Commission = percentage x sterling value ÷100

£

Step 2 Calculate the amount received in exchange by subtracting the commission from the sterling value

£

Write your answer in the box at the end of the question

Step by Step Question 2

A school arranges a trip for Year 9 in the Summer term.
The round trip is 150 miles.
3 coaches are used each of which travels 12 miles on a gallon of fuel.

> **1 gallon = 4.54 litres.**
>
> **1 litre of fuel costs 0.76p**

What is the cost of the fuel for the trip?
Give your answer to the nearest penny.

Step by step calculation

This question requires you to work out the total cost of fuel from a distance travelled in miles and a fuel consumption in miles per gallon (gal) of fuel. Use the boxes next to each step to write your answers.

To work out the total fuel consumption in gallons

Step 1 Calculate the fuel used by one coach by dividing the distance travelled by the fuel consumption per gallon

$\qquad$ gal

Step 2 Calculate the total fuel consumption by multiplying the value from step 1 by the number of coaches

Total = $\qquad$ gal

To work out the cost of fuel

Step 1 Convert the gallons to litres by multiplying the total gallons by 4.54

$\qquad$ l

Step 2 Find the cost by multiplying by the cost per litre

£ $\qquad$

Write your answer in the box at the end of the question

Question 3

A teacher was planning a lesson on measuring distance. In the teacher's dairy was a table of conversions including the following extract.

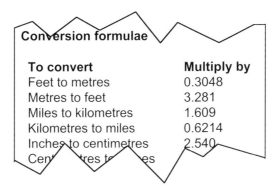

Conversion formulae	
To convert	**Multiply by**
Feet to metres	0.3048
Metres to feet	3.281
Miles to kilometres	1.609
Kilometres to miles	0.6214
Inches to centimetres	2.540
Cen... tres t... es	

From the school, it was 3.7 miles to the nearest railway station and 5.4 miles to the nearest police station.

Indicate all the true statements:

1. it is 3 kilometres to the railway station

2. it is more than 8.6 kilometres to the police station

3. the police station is exactly 2.6 kilometres further away than the railway station

Question 4

On return from a school trip to Germany, the teacher collected 20 Euros (€) from each of twelve pupils to change back into sterling. The exchange rate was 1.6€ to the pound.
Commission of 2 % was charged
How much did each pupil receive?
Give your answer to the nearest penny.

Question 5

An educational software package is listed on the internet as available in the USA, priced at $544.11 including all taxes and international delivery.
The price quoted by a British supplier is £368.00 including VAT and delivery.
The exchange rate is 1.44 dollars to the pound.

Indicate all the true statements:

1. it is cheaper to buy the software in Britain

2. the price in the USA is within £10 of the British price

3. the price in Britain is equivalent to exactly $530

Question 6

A teacher prepared the following pie chart to show parents the breakdown of costs for a planned school visit to America. The total cost of the trip is $750 per pupil. The exchange rate is £1 = $1.45

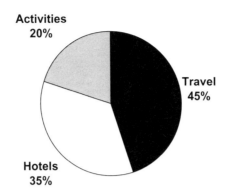

How much is the cost of travel per pupil?
Give your answer in pounds and pence.

Question 7

A teacher booked 42 places at an attraction in France at a cost of 52 French Francs per pupil.
The teacher looked up exchange rates on the internet and found the table shown below

Currency	To French Francs	In French Francs
Belgian Francs	6.14978	0.16261
Brazilian Real	0.29519	3.38763
British Pounds	0.09541	10.48059
Canadian Dollars	0.21429	4.66653
Chinese Renminbi	1.13585	0.88040

What was the total cost, in pounds sterling, of the visit to the attraction?

a. £208.38

b. £2084.10

c. £228.89

Question 8

A teacher organised a school trip to France. The teacher changed £180 into Euros (€) to pay for activities in France. The exchange rate was 1.62€ to the pound.
The teacher spent 215€ during the trip.
On returning to England, the teacher changed the unspent money into pounds at an exchange rate of 1.58€ to the pound.
How much did the teacher receive?
Give your answer to the nearest penny.

Section 10 Averages

Step by Step Question 1

A teacher analysed the end of Key Stage 3 test results in English for 5 classes.
The table shows the number of pupils in each of the 5 classes.
The bar chart shows the proportion of pupils in each class achieving Level 5 and above.

Class	A	B	C	D	E
Number of pupils	30	28	26	30	30

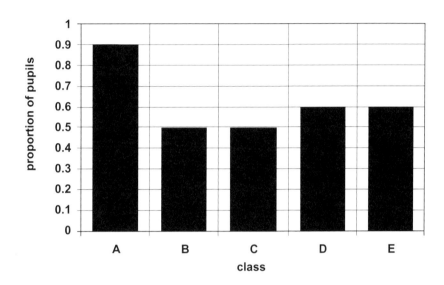

What was the mean number of pupils per class achieving Level 5 and above in English?

[ ] a. 17.5

[ ] b. 18

[ ] c. 19

Step-by-step calculation

This question requires you to calculate of the number of pupils in each class achieving Level 5 and above using the proportions in the bar chart. You also need to calculate the mean number of pupils per class achieving Level 5 and above. Use the boxes next to each step to write your answers.

To calculate the number of pupils in class A achieving Level 5 and above

Step 1 From the bar chart read off the proportion of pupils in class A achieving Level 5 and above

Step 2 Calculate the number of pupils from the proportion. Use the formula:
Number = proportion x total number of pupils in class A

To calculate the mean number of pupils in all classes achieving Level 5 and above

Step 1 Repeat steps 1 and 2 from the previous calculation for each of the classes and write your answers in the table below

Class				
A =	B =	C =	D =	E =

Step 2 Total the number of pupils calculated above

Total =

Step 3 Divide the total from step 4 by the number of classes

Mean =

Tick the box next to the correct answer

Step by Step Question 2

In an extension test for 8 pupils, one pupil achieved a mark much lower than the other pupils. The teacher calculated a median value to find a representative average performance in the test.

Pupil	A	B	C	D	E	F	G	H
Mark out of 50	31	8	29	32	29	31	29	33

Select and place the correct value in the box to show the median result for the group.

| 20.5 | 25.1 | 29 | 30 |

The median result for the group was

Step by step calculation

This question requires you to calculate the median (middle) value of a range of data. Use the boxes next to each step to write your answers.

To find the rank order

Step 1 Arrange the results in order from lowest to highest and write them in the table below. Include all 8 results.

Step 2 Draw a vertical line on the rank order (1) above, between the two values closest to the middle of the rank order, in this case the 4th and 5th value.

To find the median

Step 1 Calculate the mean of these two values in the middle of the rank order using the formula
Median = value before middle of rank + value after middle of rank ÷2

Median =

Write your answer in the box at the end of the question

Question 3

A History department gave a series of tests throughout the year. The table shows the marks for ten pupils in these tests.

	Test marks in History (marks out of 60)					
Pupil	Test 1	Test 2	Test 3	Test 4	Test 5	Mean for pupil
A	37	39	25	21	24	29.2
B	29	40	22	25	34	29.6
C	41	31	44	36	37	37.8
D	48	32	37	42	44	40.6
E	19	28	12	30	17	21.2
F	15	21	28	19	27	22.0
G	40	29	35	38	41	36.6
H	32	39	38	29	41	(1)
I	30	36	20	37	35	31.6
J	52	49	51	38	53	48.0
Range	37	28	39	23	(2)	

Select and write the correct values in the boxes (1) and (2) to complete the table.

35.7	35.8	35.9
24	27	36

Question 4

The table shows the French GCSE grades achieved by a group of pupils and the points score for each grade.

	GCSE grades achieved in French								
GCSE Grade	A*	A	B	C	D	E	F	G	U
Number of pupils achieving each grade	1	4	5	6	4	3	3	2	2
Points score for each grade	8	7	6	5	4	3	2	1	0

The mean GCSE points score can be calculated using the formula:

$$\text{Mean GCSE points score} = \frac{\text{Total points score}}{\text{Total number of pupils}}$$

What was the mean GCSE points score for French?

Question 5

A Secondary school teacher prepared a box and whisker graph to show the range of marks achieved by the tutor group in the end of term tests.

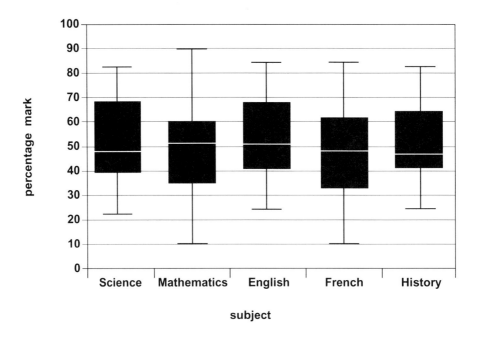

Circle the subject where the median mark was less than 50 % and the range of marks was greater than 70 %.

Question 6

The table shows the authorised and unauthorised absences for three classes over a six-week period.

	Number of 1/2 day absences					
	Class A (30) pupils		Class B (28) pupils)		Class C (30) pupils	
Week	Authorised	Unauthorised	Authorised	Unauthorised	Authorised	Unauthorised
1	28	22	22	12	24	13
2	49	32	10	18	9	10
3	17	10	25	15	24	8
4	25	45	16	8	40	21
5	24	20	18	12	30	25
6	36	12	23	13	24	12

Indicate all the true statements:

1. class B had the least total number of unauthorised absences

2. the mean number of authorised absences in week 4 was 27 per class

3. the greatest range of authorised absences was in class C

Question 7

The table shows the GCSE grades achieved in Geography by pupils in three classes.

Grade	Number of pupils achieving each grade		
	Class 1	Class 2	Class 3
A*	2	4	0
A	4	6	4
B	6	4	6
C	4	8	6
D	7	2	10
E	3	1	2
F	2	3	1
G	2	2	1
Total	30	30	30

What was the mean number of pupils achieving grades A* - C?

☐ a. 16

☐ b. 18

☐ c. 19

Question 8

A survey was carried out of homework done on one day by 8 pupils in a Year 7 class.
The results for 8 pupils from one teacher's class are shown in table 1.

Table 1

Pupil	A	B	C	D	E	F	G	H
Time spent (minutes)	20	40	10	40	60	30	0	40
Questions completed	3	11	1	5	15	3	0	9
Words written	25	150	25	75	250	25	0	75

Circle the number of the column in table 2 that shows the results for this class.

Table 2

	1	2	3	4	5	6
Mode of time spent (minutes)	60	30	40	30	35	40
Mode of number of questions completed	15	5.9	3	6	4	4
Mode of words written	250	78	25	80	50	25

Section 11 Formulae

Step by Step Question 1

The table shows the points score for end of Key Stage 2 Mathematics Levels in 2000.

Level achieved	N	2	3	4	5	6
Points score	15	15	21	27	33	39

A school's end of Key Stage 2 results in Mathematics are listed below.

> **1 pupil achieved N**
> **4 pupils achieved Level 2**
> **7 pupils achieved Level 3**
> **10 pupils achieved Level 4**
> **6 pupils achieved Level 5**

The school's mean points score is calculated using the formula:

> **Mean points score = total points score ÷ total number of pupils**

What was the school's mean points score?
Give your answer to one decimal place.

Step by step calculation

This question requires you to work out a mean by first working out and adding together the points scored by the pupils at each Level. Use the boxes next to each step to write your answers.

To work out the points score for Level 5

Step 1 Look up the number of points for Level 5 from the table

Step 2 Multiply this by the number of pupils achieving Level 5.
Transfer this value to the table below

To work out the mean points score

Step 1 Repeat the previous calculation for each of the Levels

Level				
5 =	4 =	3 =	2 =	N =

Step 2 Find the total points score by adding the points score for each of the Levels

Step 3 Calculate the mean points score by dividing the total points score by the number of pupils

Write your answer in the box at the end of the question.

Step by Step Question 2

To work out GCSE coursework marks, a Head of Department provided teachers with the following formula:

> **Total mark = [(skill A + skill B + skill C + skill D) x 2] + QL**

The table shows marks gained by 3 pupils in their coursework.

Pupil	Skill A	Skill B	Skill C	Skill D	QL	Total mark
A	9	6	5	3	2	(1)
B	6	2	4	2	2	30
C	8	5	6	4	3	(2)

Select and write the correct total coursework marks in the boxes (**1**) and (**2**) to complete the table.

46	48	49	51

Step by step calculation

In this question you are required to use a formula involving addition and multiplication to work out total marks. Use the boxes next to each step to write your answers.

To work out the course work marks of each pupil

Step 1 Add the number of marks for each of the skills A – D for pupil A

Skills mark
=

Step 2 Multiply this mark by 2

=

Step 3 Add the QL mark

Total =

Select the correct value from the numbers in the boxes and write it in box 1 in the table.

Step 4 Repeat steps 1, 2 and 3 for pupil C

Skills mark
=

=

Total =

Select the correct value from the numbers in the boxes and write it in box 2 in the table

Question 3

Using data provided by the LEA, the head teacher prepared a formula to allow teachers to predict likely achievement in end of Key Stage 2 English assessments from the pupil's achievement in end of Key Stage 1 English assessments.

> **Predicted end of Key Stage 2 English Level = (end of Key Stage 1 Level x 1.1) + 0.9**

What is the predicted end of Key Stage 2 English Level for a pupil who achieved Level 3 in the end of Key Stage 1 English assessments? Give your answer to the nearest whole number.

☐	a. 3
☐	b. 4
☐	c. 5

Question 4

A teacher was planning an extension lesson about volume for a group of Year 6 pupils. The teacher checked the answer to a problem set.
The formula for calculating volume of a cylinder is

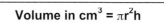

Volume in cm^3 = $\pi r^2 h$

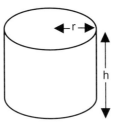

π = 3.142
r = the radius
h = the height

A cylinder was given

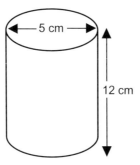

5 cm

12 cm

What is the volume of the cylinder?

☐	a. 94.26 cm^3
☐	b. 235.65 cm^3
☐	c. 942.60 cm^3

Question 5

As part of a project about weather, a teacher collected various thermometers, some measuring in °C, some in °F. The teacher prepared a worksheet about conversions from °F to °C. The teacher checked the sums before the lesson.

The formula for converting °F to °C is:

> **Temperature in °C = (temperature in °F – 32) x 0.45**

What is the correct temperature in °C for a temperature of 24°F?

☐ a. - 3.6°C

☐ b. - 8.0°C

☐ c. - 17.7°C

Question 6

A teacher plans a class activity to measure the height of some trees. The teacher found a formula in a book and tried it out before the lesson.
The formula was:

> **Height of tree in metres = (tangent of angle x distance from tree) + height of eyes of user**

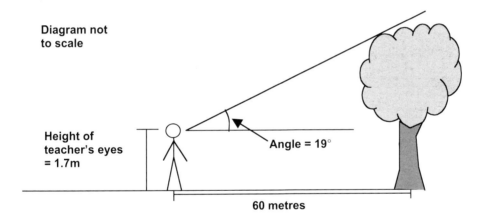

Diagram not to scale

Height of teacher's eyes = 1.7m

Angle = 19°

60 metres

Using a calculator, the teacher found that the tangent of angle 19° = 0.344.

What was the height of the tree the teacher used to test the formula, to the nearest whole metre?

Question 7

A head teacher uses a formula to work out financial allocations to departments. The formula is:

> **Allocation = number of pupils in Year groups x amount of money per pupil**

Table 1 shows the money allocated per pupil in different Year groups.

Table 1

Year groups	Amount of money per pupil (£)		
	Art and Technology	Humanities	Science and Maths
7, 8 and 9	1.50	1.25	1.75
10 and 11	2.00	1.75	2.50
12 and 13	3.50	3.00	4.00

Table 2 shows the number of pupils from each year group in each department.

Table 2

Year groups	Number of pupils from each Year group in each department		
	Art and Technology	Humanities	Science and Maths
7, 8 and 9	300	300	300
10 and 11	120	200	200
12 and 13	45	80	70

Which department receives £725 for Years 7 to 11?

☐ a. Art and Technology

☐ b. Humanities

☐ c. Science and Maths

Question 8

A teacher calculated coursework marks for a GCSE course. The teacher's curriculum manager provided the following formulae:

> **For complex tasks: total mark = [A+B+C+D] x 2+SPAG**

> **For simple tasks: total mark = [(A/1.5)+B+C+D] x 2+SPAG**

Pupil	Complexity of task	A	B	C	D	SPAG
L	Simple	4	2	2	1	1
M	Complex	9	5	6	4	3
N	Simple	12	6	6	4	2

Circle the letter of the pupil who had a total mark of 50.

Chapter 4   Skills Practice - Mental

This chapter provides you with a large number of varied mental arithmetic questions in each of the areas tested in the QTS Numeracy Skills Test. These questions are in addition to those on the CD. Together they provide practice in the skills of mental arithmetic.

Find someone else to read them to you. Ask the person to read the question clearly, pause and read it again. You are then allowed 18 seconds before the next question. If you are unable to find anyone to help use a piece of paper to cover the questions and uncover them one at a time.

The audio CD consists of seven, timed practice tests. Each test has a practice question followed 12 others. Combined with the written practice tests in Chapter 5, this provides the opportunity to simulate the test in full. The questions in this chapter and the questions on the CD together will enable you to develop confidence and competence in dealing with the full range of mental arithmetic questions.

The answers to all the questions can be found in Chapter 6.

The mental arithmetic part of the test is for many, the most demanding section of the test. You will rarely be in a situation comparable to this and in addition, the timed element of the test leaves no room for any lack of concentration. Unlike the written part of the test, you have no opportunity to go back to a question.

Tips for answering mental arithmetic questions:

➤   concentrate – the mental arithmetic test only lasts approximately ten minutes

➤   listen carefully

➤   don't panic if you don't hear or don't understand a question. It will be repeated, and if you still don't get it, then clear your head for the next one

➤   use a piece of paper to write down the sum that you are being asked to calculate. (In the live test, you will be provided with a piece of paper)

➤   take your time

➤   if you finish a question quickly, relax and clear your head while you wait for the next question.

Section 1   Time

Question 1

A school party travels in a minibus to a heritage site sixty miles away. The average speed of the minibus is thirty six miles per hour. How long will it take to reach the heritage site?

Question 2

Lessons in a school last for one hour and twenty minutes. The afternoon session begins at thirteen fifteen and has two lessons. At what time does the afternoon session end?

Question 3

A GCSE examination was one hour and fifteen minutes long. A pupil arrived eighteen minutes late.
How much time did the pupil have for the examination? Give your answer in minutes.

Question 4

A school day starts at eight fifty and ends at fifteen fifty. Lunch lasts one hour and there is a twenty minute morning break. How much time is available for teaching? Give your answer in hours and minutes.

Question 5

A topic is allocated three lessons of forty five minutes each. The teacher plans to use one hundred and ten minutes for various tasks. How much time is available for a test?

Question 6

After school games practice lasts forty five minutes. Ten minutes is needed for the teams to change before and after. The school day ends at fifteen forty. At what time will the teams leave school?

Question 7

The air flight time for a school skiing trip is two hours and fifty minutes. The flight departs at local time fifteen thirty. Local time at the destination is one hour ahead.
At what local time is the plane expected to land at its destination?

Question 8

The contact time for a teacher is twenty hours per week. Each lesson is forty minutes.
How many lessons per week does the teacher have?

Section 2 Money

Question 1
A teacher ordered equipment worth four hundred and fifty five pounds. The supplier gave a discount of ten percent. How much did the order cost after the discount?

Question 2
A teacher orders six microscopes costing one hundred and twenty pounds each. A ten per cent discount is given. What is the cost of the order after the discount?

Question 3
A teacher spends a total of eighty five pounds on printing and colour photocopying.
Printing costs are four fifths of the total. How much is spent on colour photocopying?

Question 4
A teacher attends a training course and claims travelling expenses at the rate of thirty pence per mile. The total claim is fifteen pounds sixty pence. How many miles did the teacher travel?

Question 5
A Geography department has one hundred and fifty textbooks. One fifth need replacing. The cost of new textbooks is seven pounds ninety pence each. What is the cost of replacing the textbooks?

Question 6
A department budget has sixty nine pounds left to spend before the year end.
How many dictionaries costing three pounds forty five each can be purchased?

Question 7
Three quarters of the cost of a school visit is for travel. The whole visit costs twenty six pounds per person. What is the cost of travel per person?

Question 8
A publisher will give a fifteen percent discount if more than two hundred pounds is spent. A textbook costs five pounds twenty. What is the minimum number of textbooks that must be purchased to receive a discount?

Section 3   Proportions, fractions and decimals

Question 1
A year group of eight classes has two hundred and forty pupils.
Three fifths of the pupils are girls. Each class has an equal number of girls.
How many girls are there in each class?

Question 2
During an Ofsted inspection of a Primary school, five eighths of the seventy two lessons observed were judged as satisfactory. How many lessons were judged as satisfactory?

Question 3
What is nought point seven five of one hundred and sixty four?

Question 4
A teacher teaches thirty six periods of equal length in a week.
Six are spent teaching History, twelve teaching Humanities and the remainder teaching Geography.
What fraction of the teacher's teaching time is spent teaching Geography?

Question 5
Four ninths of a Year group are boys.
How many boys are there in a year group of one hundred and twenty six?

Question 6
Three fifths of a Year group of one hundred and sixty five pupils achieved grades A star to C in English.
How many pupils achieved grades A star to C?

Question 7
In a school of five hundred and twenty, five eighths are girls.
How many boys are there in the school?

Question 8
A Year group choose between three subject options, A, B and C. Nought point two three of the group choose option A. Nought point three seven of the group choose option B.
What proportion of the group chose option C? Give your answer as a decimal.

Section 4 Percentages

Question 1

A school sells two hundred and fifty tickets for the first night of a school play.
On the first night ninety per cent of the ticket holders attend. How many people attend the first night?

```
```

Question 2

A pupil scores forty five out of sixty in a test. The teacher sets the pupil a target of increasing his test score by five percentage points in the next test which is marked out of fifty.
What is the minimum mark the pupil needs to score to achieve the target?

```
```

Question 3

One hundred and sixty pupils sit GCSE English and Mathematics.
Seventy two pupils achieve a grade C in English and fifty six achieve a grade C in Mathematics.
What is the difference in the percentage achieving a grade C in the two subjects?

```
```

Question 4

A school band has seventeen pupils from Year eight, thirteen pupils from Year nine and twenty pupils from Year ten. The school has a total of two hundred and fifty pupils.
What percentage of the school is in the school band?

```
```

Question 5

The test result of one pupil is twenty four out of forty. The test result of another pupil is thirty six out of forty. What is the difference in the percentages achieved by the pupils?

```
```

Question 6

The mean mark for a class test was forty five out of sixty.
What is this as a percentage?

```
```

Question 7

In a test, a pupil achieved fifteen out of fifty. On retaking the test, the pupil achieved thirty five out of fifty.
By how many percentage points had the pupil improved?

```
```

Question 8

A pupil is absent from twelve out of twenty lessons. Over the next twenty lessons, the pupil misses ten lessons. What is the improvement in attendance as a percentage?

```
```

Section 5   Measurements

Question 1
A classroom is four metres by four point five metres. A computer suite occupies an area of six square metres. What fraction of the classroom can be used for desks?

Question 2
A school science laboratory has six benches measuring two metres by nought point eight metres. What is the total area of bench space available? Give your answer in square metres.

Question 3
Twenty five pupils in an art class each need four strips of coloured tape.
Each strip of coloured tape is three centimetres long. How many metres of tape will be needed?

Question 4
A Mathematics class count three hundred strides as the distance across the school playing fields. A stride covers seventy five centimetres. What is the distance in metres across the playing fields?

Question 5
A Drama teacher orders fabric to make twelve cloaks. Each cloak uses a one metre width and one and a half metre length of fabric. The fabric is sold in two metre widths. How many metres of fabric does the teacher order?

Question 6
New blinds are needed for four windows each measuring one point five metres by two metres. What is the total area to be covered? Give your answer in square metres.

Question 7
A teacher needs a solution containing twelve grams of salt per litre of solution. How many grams of salt will the teacher use to make two hundred and fifty centimetres cubed of this solution?

Question 8
A school play area measures fifty metres by thirty metres. One fifth of this is used for a five-a-side football pitch. What is the area of the football pitch in square metres?

Section 6 Conversions

Question 1
One kilometre is equal to nought point six two miles.
A school minibus travels one hundred and fifty kilometres on a school trip.
How many miles does the minibus travel?

Question 2
On returning from a trip to Germany, a teacher had forty eight euros left. At an exchange rate of one point six euros to the pound, how many pounds would the teacher receive?

Question 3
Convert three fifths to a decimal

Question 4
A Science investigation needs five grams of sugar per pupil. Science classes each have twenty five pupils. How many classes will be supplied by a one kilogram bag of sugar?

Question 5
The scale of a map used in Geography lesson is two centimetres for every five miles.
The distance on the map between the school and the town centre is three centimetres.
How many miles is the school from the town centre?

Question 6
The tables used to display pupil's work for an open day are two hundred centimetres long by seventy five centimetres wide. What is the area of each table? Give your answer in square metres.

Question 7
Twenty pupils each need seventy five cubic centimetres of liquid for an experiment.
What is the total volume of liquid needed for the class? Give your answer in litres.

Question 8
The school orchestra travels one thousand six hundred and twenty kilometres during a tour of France.
There are one point six two kilometres in a mile. How many miles does the school orchestra travel?

Section 7 Arithmetical processes

Question 1
A school party consists of fifteen adults and eight classes each of twenty eight pupils.
How many fifty-two seat coaches will be needed for the party?

_____

Question 2
From a Year group of one hundred and twenty seven pupils, ninety seven achieve Level five and above in end of Key Stage three English. How many do not achieve Level five?

_____

Question 3
One hundred and sixty eight pupils are time-tabled to have an English lesson at the same time on Thursday. Each class has twenty eight pupils. How many English teachers are needed?

_____

Question 4
A Science laboratory has four computers. Each pupil is allowed ten minutes on a computer.
What is the maximum number of pupils that can use a computer in a one hour lesson?

_____

Question 5
Fifty-six pupils take part in a nativity play. Eight pupils are needed for main roles.
The remainder of the pupils are to be split equally into shepherds, angels and animals.
How many pupils will be shepherds?

_____

Question 6
An examination room has space for one hundred and thirty pupils. Classrooms have space for fifteen pupils. How many extra classrooms will be needed for an examination entry of one hundred and seventy pupils?

_____

Question 7
Twenty percent of Year four pupils and ten percent of Year five pupils are in the school band.
There are one hundred and fifty pupils in Year four and one hundred and eighty pupils in Year five.
How many pupils are there in the band?

_____

Question 8
A school books three ninety-six seat buses for a visit. On the day, one of the buses is full and the other two are three-quarters full. How many people are on the buses?

_____

Chapter 5 Practice Tests

The Numeracy test has two components: section 1 - Mental arithmetic and section 2 - On-screen questions. The mental arithmetic section of the test can be found on the CD. The on-screen (written) section of the test is provided in this chapter. The CD has seven mental arithmetic sections. The book has two on-screen (written) sections. These can be combined to provide a complete simulation of the Numeracy Skills Test. They may also be used with the mental arithmetic questions in Chapter 4.

A blank answer grid for use with these tests can be found in appendix 2.

Practice Test 1

Question 1

The table shows the number of GCSE entries for five subjects in a school.
The bar chart shows the percentage of pupils achieving GCSE grades A* - C in the subjects in 2001.

GCSE subject	Drama	Music	P.E.	Geography	History
Total number of GCSE entries	60	40	44	60	80

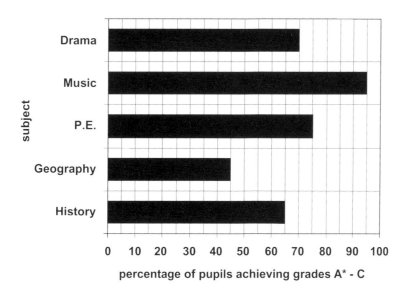

percentage of pupils achieving grades A* - C

Indicate all the true statements:

1. 20 pupils did not achieve a grade A* - C. in Drama

2. twice as many pupils achieved a grade A* - C in History as in Geography

3. more pupils achieved a grade A* - C in History than in Music

Question 2

A school trip consists of a total of 158 pupils from 5 classes and their class tutors.
The pupil teacher ratio for the trip needs to be 1 to 12.
How many more adults are needed?

Question 3

The table shows the number of pupils in Year 9 in a school from 1996 to 2000.

Year	1996	1997	1998	1999	2000
Number of pupils in Year 9	164	156	178	185	175

The bar chart shows the proportion of pupils in the school choosing Drama as a GCSE subject at the end of Year 9 from 1996 to 2000.

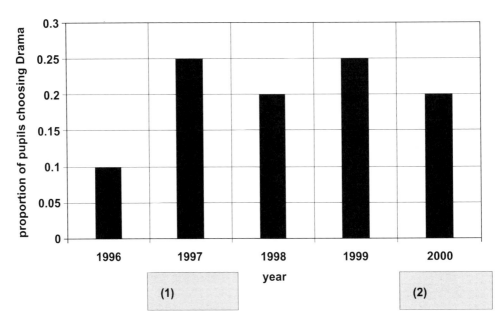

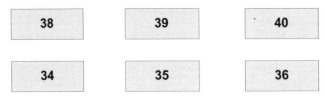

Select and write the correct values in the boxes **(1)** and **(2)** to show the number of pupils choosing Drama in 1997 and 2000.

38	39	40
34	35	36

Question 4

During a school trip a minibus travelled 250 kilometres. The average fuel consumption for the minibus is 31 miles per gallon. How many litres of fuel did the minibus use during the trip?
Give your answer to the nearest litre.

> 1 kilometre = 0.62 miles.
> 1 gallon = 4.54 litres.

Question 5

In a school there are 1080 pupils. During a staff meeting on curriculum enrichment the head teacher gave out a table showing the number of pupils studying various subjects.

Subject	German	Italian	Business	Media	Psychology
Number of pupils	216	108	180	43	135

Which of the following is true?

- a. 1/4 of pupils are studying German
- b. 1/10 of pupils are studying Media
- c. 1/8 of pupils are studying Psychology
- d. 1/6 of pupils are studying Italian

Question 6

The table shows the actual age and reading age for a group of Year 7 pupils.

Pupil	Actual age (years - months)	Reading age (years - months)
A	10 - 8	12 - 3
B	11 - 6	10 - 8
C	11 - 10	12 - 5
D	9 - 6	10 - 7
E	9 - 11	9 - 5
F	11 - 0	10 - 3
G	12 - 6	11 - 9
H	12 - 3	11 - 7
I	10 - 9	9 - 11
J	10 - 3	11 - 4

Circle the letters of the pupils who had a difference between their actual age and their reading age greater then 12 months.

Question 7

A teacher travelled to a training course by public transport. The teacher travelled by bus to the station at a cost of £1.20. The return train fare was £27.95. The taxi cost £4.41 from the station to the venue, and the same fare to return to the station. On the way back to the station, the cost of the taxi was shared between three people. The bus home from the station again cost £1.20.

The teacher calculated the cost of travel for the day, to be claimed back from the school's training budget. What was the cost of the travel for the day?

a. £36.23

b. £39.17

c. £64.18

Question 8

A teacher is installing a new piece of software.
The diagram shows the options available and their size in megabytes (MB).

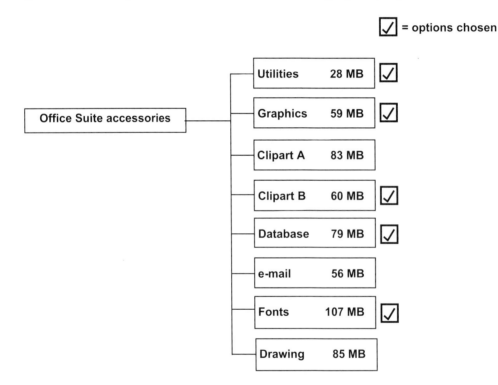

The computer can install the software at the rate of 1.85 MB in 15 seconds.
How long will it take to install all the options chosen?
Give your answer in minutes.

Question 9

The graph shows the cumulative frequency of end of Key Stage 3 Levels in Science for pupils at a school.

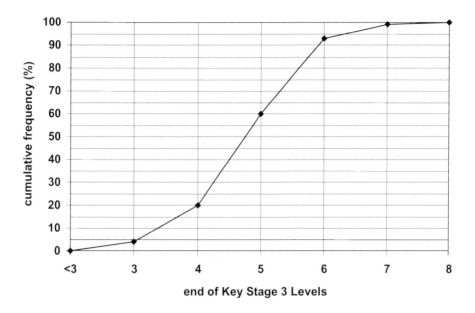

What percentage of pupils achieved Level 4 or above at the end of Key Stage 3?

a. 20 %

b. 80 %

c. 95 %

Question 10

The table shows the coursework marks achieved by a group of eleven pupils

Pupil	A	B	C	D	E	F	G	H	I	J	K
Mark out of 65	53	45	34	45	38	56	60	56	53	45	50

Indicate all the true statements:

1. the mode for this group is 45

2. the mean mark is 44

3. the range of marks is 26

Question 11

In an attempt to improve attendance, a teacher analysed the attendance for five Year 10 classes over a year. This analysis is shown in the bar chart.

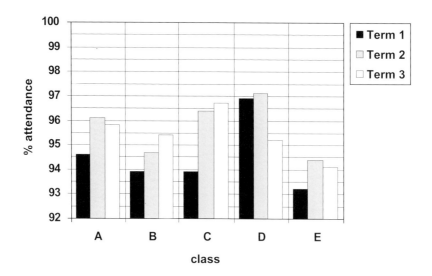

Indicate all the true statements:

1. the highest attendance in term 3 was in class A

2. the total number of absences in term 2 was highest in class E

3. all classes improved their attendance from term 1 to term 2

Question 12

The mean end of Key Stage 3 points score for a school is calculated using the formula:

> **mean points score = total points score**
> **total number of pupils**

In 2000, a school had a mean points score of 35.1, and in 2001, a mean points score of 36.3.
One hundred and sixty pupils took the end of Key Stage assessments in both years.
What was the difference in the school's total points score in 2000 and 2001?

Question 13

At a staff meeting to discuss reading performance, a head teacher gave out a box and whisker diagram showing reading ages of pupils in Year 6 at four local schools.

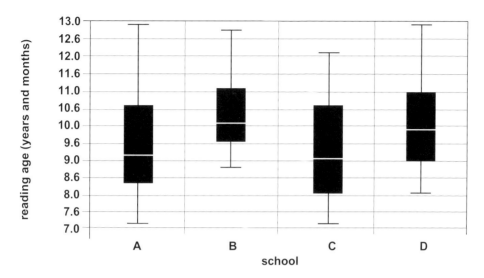

Indicate all the true statements:

1. school D had the lowest upper quartile value

2. the range for school A was greater than the range for any of the other schools

3. the median reading age was lowest in school C

Question 14

At a staff meeting about reading, the head teacher gave out the following pie charts. The pie charts show the percentage of pupils in Year 4 with different reading ages from 1997 to 2000.

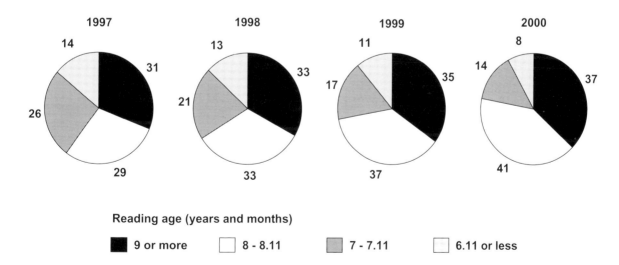

In 2001, there will be 40 pupils in Year 4. Assuming current trends continue, what will be the number of pupils in Year 4 with reading ages between 8 and 8.11?

Question 15

A class measured the rainfall for a week using the school's weather monitor. The table shows the daily record.

Rainfall (mm)					
Monday	Tuesday	Wednesday	Thursday	Friday	Weekend
2.0	1.5	17.8	0	0.7	10.2

What was the total rainfall for the week?

☐ a. 322 mm

☐ b. 32.2 cm

☐ c. 3.22 cm

Question 16

A Geography teacher made estimates of GCSE grades based on pupil's mock examination results. The table shows the estimates.

Mock examination score (%)	less than 45	45 - 54	55 - 64	65 - 72	73 - 79	80 - 85	86+
Estimated GCSE grade	G or F	E	D	C	B	A	A*

The scatter graph shows the mock examination scores and the actual GCSE grade for eleven pupils.

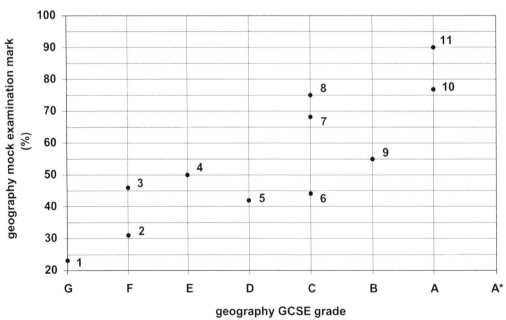

Circle the numbers of the pupils who gained a GCSE grade C or above and whose actual GCSE grade was better than their estimated grade.

Practice Test 2

Question 1

The diagram shows an extract from an attendance register over a three-week period.

	Week 1					Week 2					Week 3				
Pupil	M	T	W	T	F	M	T	W	T	F	M	T	W	T	F
A															
B															
C															
D															
E															
F															
G															
H															
I															
J															

∕ = present am   ＼ = present pm   ◯ = absent

Indicate all the true statements:

1. pupil E had most absences

2. pupil D had a 80% attendance rate over the 3 weeks

3. pupils A and F had the same number of absences

4. 4 pupils had an attendance rate of 95% or more

Question 2

A teacher wished to average some test results for use in a report. For one particular pupil, a few of the test results were exceptionally poor due to personal problems. The teacher decided to use the median rather than the mean as a measure of the average test result for the pupil.

Test	1	2	3	4	5	6	7	8	9	10
Mark out of 80	58	65	11	15	17	71	61	58	59	66

What was the median test mark for the pupil?

Question 3

The table shows the test marks for five pupils in Spanish.

Pupil	Test marks in Spanish			
	Test 1 (out of 40)	Test 2 (out of 50)	Test 3 (out of 100)	Test 4 (out of 75)
A	34	25	48	49
B	28	32	65	48
C	27	28	72	59
D	19	24	53	42
E	28	35	70	64

In which two tests did pupil B score the same percentage mark?

a. 1 and 2

b. 2 and 4

c. 2 and 3

Question 4

The head teacher of a Primary school prepared the following graph showing the pre-school experience of pupils admitted to school.

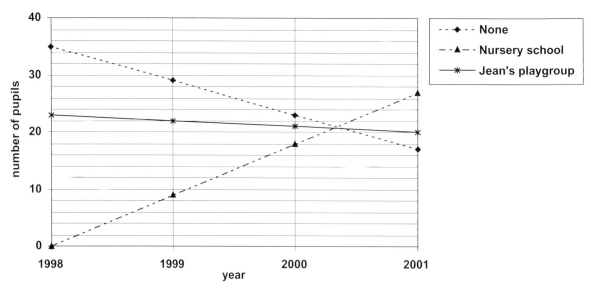

Circle the letter (**P**, **Q**, or **R**) in the table below that shows the pre-school experience of pupils admitted in 2002 if recent trends continue.

	Number of pupils admitted in 2002		
Pre-school experience	P	Q	R
None	10	17	11
Nursery school	37	27	36
Jean's playgroup	18	30	19

Question 5

The head teacher of a school produced a bar chart comparing reading ages at three local schools.

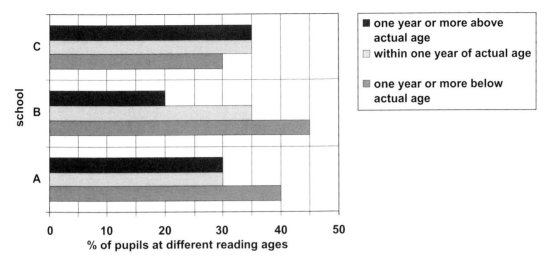

Indicate all the true statements:

1. school A had a higher percentage of pupils with reading ages one year or more below their actual age than school C

2. school B had the biggest difference between the percentage of pupils with reading ages one year or more below and one year or more above their actual age

3. for pupils with reading ages one year or more above their actual age, school A had a higher percentage of pupils than school B or school C

Question 6

As part of a Technology project, pupils are using sheets of plastic measuring 30 cm by 18 cm. Each pupil requires 2 sheets of plastic.

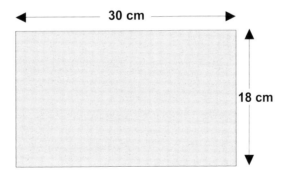

6 classes each of 18 pupils are involved in the project.
The plastic is purchased in large sheets measuring 1m by 1m, which is cut to the required size.
How many large sheets will be needed for the project?

Question 7

The graph shows the percentage of pupils in a school achieving Level 4 and above in end of Key Stage 2 English from 1996 to 2000.

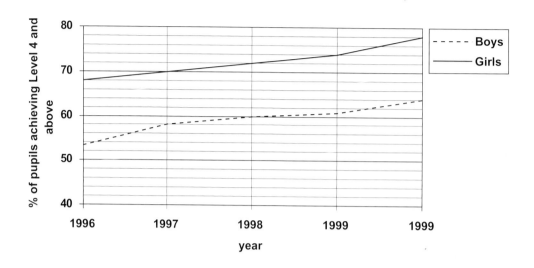

In which two years was the percentage difference in performance between boys and girls the same?

☐ a. 1996 and 1997

☐ b. 1997 and 1998

☐ c. 1997 and 1999

☐ d. 1999 and 2000

Question 8

A class sat a series of tests. To work out a final mark, the teacher used a formula:

> **(Test 1 mark x 0.8) + (Test 2 mark x 0.6) + Test 3 mark**

The table shows the test marks for three pupils.

Pupil	Test 1 mark	Test 2 mark	Test 3 mark	Final mark
A	27	41	23	69.2
B	35	28	26	**(1)**
C	21	35	26	**(2)**

Select and write the correct values for the final mark for pupils B and C in the boxes **(1)** and **(2)**.

| 57.1 | 59.6 | 63.8 |

| 70.8 | 82.0 | 89.0 |

Question 9

A head teacher produced a cumulative frequency graph summarising responses to a question about ICT facilities completed by 180 pupils.

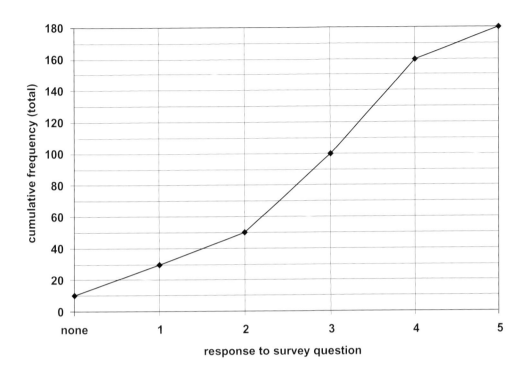

How many pupils gave a response between 1 and 4 on this questionnaire?

☐ a. 130

☐ b. 150

☐ c. 160

Question 10

A Science department has 185 pupils in Year 11.
The department produces a mock examination paper consisting of 24 pages for each pupil.
The cost of printing is 1.75 pence per page.

How much will it cost to produce all the mock examination papers?
Give your answer in pounds and pence.

Question 11

The table shows the grades achieved in GCSE Science and Mathematics by a group of pupils.

GCSE Grade in Science	GCSE grade in Mathematics								
	A*	A	B	C	D	E	F	G	U
A*	1	1	1						
A	1	1		1					
B	1		1	1					
C			2	1	3				
D				1	2	2		1	
E				1		2	1	1	
F						1		1	
G								1	
U									1

What proportion of the pupils achieved grades A* to C in both subjects?

☐ a. 40 %

☐ b. 47 %

☐ c. 50 %

Question 12

The diagram shows two footpaths in the grounds of a local historic house that is being used for a fundraising activity. A pupil walks footpath 1 three times and footpath 2 one and a half times. The pupil is sponsored at 50 pence per kilometre by five people and 75 pence per kilometre by ten people.

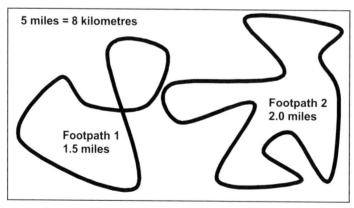

5 miles = 8 kilometres

Footpath 2
2.0 miles

Footpath 1
1.5 miles

Indicate all of the true statements.

☐ 1. the pupil walks a total of 12 kilometres

☐ 2. the pupil raises a total of £130

☐ 3. to raise £150, the pupil needs 5 more sponsors at 50 pence per kilometre

Question 13

A teacher was given a scatter graph showing how pupils from two different groups had performed in their end of Key Stage 2 and 3 Assessments. Mean Levels had been calculated for each pupil from their results in English, Mathematics and Science.

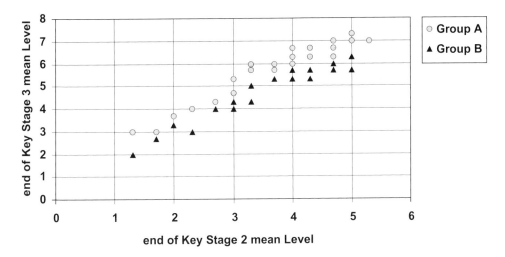

Indicate all the true statements:

1. two pupils who achieved Level 3 or less at the end of Key Stage 2 achieved higher than Level 5 in end of Key Stage 3

2. group A achieved greater improvement from end of Key Stage 2 to end of Key Stage 3 than group B

3. in group B, no pupils gained a Level 6 and above in the end of Key Stage 3 tests

Question 14

A Mathematics department made estimates of the number of pupils expected to achieve each grade in GCSE Mathematics. The bar chart shows the estimated results and the actual results for the 175 pupils.

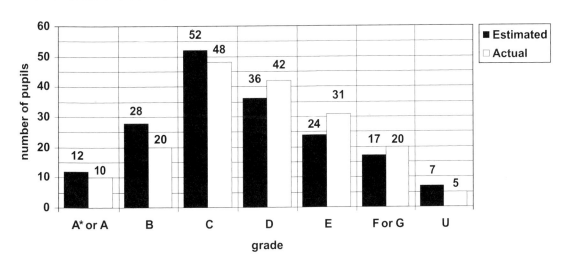

What was the difference between the percentage of estimated grades A* - C and the actual percentage of grades A* - C?

Question 15

A teacher prepared a pie chart to illustrate the use of time during a 32 hour 30 minute school week for a Year 2 class.

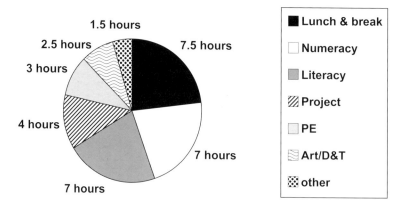

Literacy and Numeracy were to be spread evenly across four days.

How long would be spent on Literacy and Numeracy together on each of the four days?

	a. 3 hours 12 minutes
	b. 3 hours 30 minutes
	c. 1 hour 45 minutes

Question 16

The bar chart shows the number of pupils in a Primary school achieving different Levels in end of Key Stage 1 Mathematics.

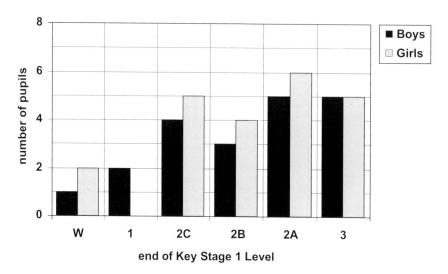

What proportion of boys achieved Level 3?
Give your answer as a decimal.

Chapter 6 Answers

Skills Practice - Written

Interpreting and using statistical information

Section 1 Identify trends correctly		Section 2 Make Comparisons and draw conclusions	
Question 1	c	Question 1	1 and 3
Question 2	1 only	Question 2	1 and 3
Question 3	a	Question 3	1 and 2
Question 4	c	Question 4	1, 2 and 3
Question 5	3 only	Question 5	1 and 3
Question 6	1 and 3	Question 6	1, 2 and 3
Question 7	1, 2 and 3	Question 7	History
Question 8	Test Z	Question 8	1 and 2

Section 3 Interpretation of Data

Question 1	2 and 3
Question 2	Pupil 3
Question 3	3 only
Question 4	1 only
Question 5	b
Question 6	1 and 3
Question 7	1 and 2
Question 8	1071

Using and applying general arithmetic

Section 4 Time		Section 5 Money	
Question 1	C	Question 1	1 and 3
Question 2	18 h 40 m	Question 2	£38.06
Question 3	14:35	Question 3	C and D
Question 4	4 h 40 m	Question 4	£247.00
Question 5	9 h 30 m	Question 5	£1455.00
Question 6	34 h 10 m	Question 6	a
Question 7	1	Question 7	£116.00
Question 8	16:20	Question 8	£673.90

Section 6 Proportion and ratio
Question 1	1 = 23, 2 = 0.15
Question 2	4:5
Question 3	4:3
Question 4	1 and 3
Question 5	C
Question 6	2000
Question 7	Y
Question 8	b

Section 7 Percentages, fractions and decimals
Question 1	1 and 3
Question 2	84
Question 3	2 and 3
Question 4	5
Question 5	59
Question 6	b
Question 7	1 = 93, 2 = 5.71 %
Question 8	c

Section 8 Measurements
Question 1	6.5 m^2
Question 2	1 and 3
Question 3	b
Question 4	81
Question 5	c
Question 6	C
Question 7	B and Z
Question 8	c

Section 9 Conversions
Question 1	£46.26
Question 2	£129.39
Question 3	2 only
Question 4	£12.25
Question 5	1 and 2
Question 6	£232.76
Question 7	a
Question 8	£48.48

Section 10 Averages
Question 1	b
Question 2	30
Question 3	1 = 35.8, 2 = 36
Question 4	4.3
Question 5	French
Question 6	1 and 2
Question 7	b
Question 8	3

Section 11 Formulae
Question 1	24.6
Question 2	1 = 48, 2 = 49
Question 3	b
Question 4	b
Question 5	a
Question 6	22
Question 7	b
Question 8	N

Skills Practice – Mental

Section 1 Time
Question 1	1 h 40 m
Question 2	15:55
Question 3	57 m
Question 4	5 h 40 m
Question 5	25 m
Question 6	16:45
Question 7	19:20
Question 8	30

Section 2 Money
Question 1	£409.50
Question 2	£648.00
Question 3	£17.00
Question 4	52
Question 5	£237.00
Question 6	20
Question 7	£19.50
Question 8	39

Section 3 Proportions, fractions, decimals

Question 1	18
Question 2	45
Question 3	123
Question 4	1/2
Question 5	56
Question 6	99
Question 7	195
Question 8	0.4

Section 4 Percentages

Question 1	225
Question 2	40
Question 3	10 %
Question 4	20 %
Question 5	30 %
Question 6	75 %
Question 7	40
Question 8	10

Section 5 Measurements

Question 1	2/3
Question 2	9.6 m^2
Question 3	3 m
Question 4	225 m
Question 5	9 m
Question 6	12 m^2
Question 7	3 g
Question 8	300 m^2

Section 6 Conversions

Question 1	93
Question 2	£30.00
Question 3	0.6
Question 4	8
Question 5	7.5 m
Question 6	1.5 m^2
Question 7	1.5 l
Question 8	1000 m

Section 7 Arithmetical Processes

Question 1	5
Question 2	30
Question 3	6
Question 4	24
Question 5	16
Question 6	3
Question 7	48
Question 8	240

Written Practice Test 1

Question 1	3 only
Question 2	9
Question 3	1 = 39, 2 = 35
Question 4	23
Question 5	c
Question 6	A, D and J
Question 7	a
Question 8	45 m
Question 9	c
Question 10	1 and 3
Question 11	2 and 3
Question 12	192
Question 13	2 and 3
Question 14	18
Question 15	c
Question 16	6, 9, 10

Written Practice Test 2

Question 1	1, 2 and 3
Question 2	58.5
Question 3	b
Question 4	R
Question 5	1 and 2
Question 6	15
Question 7	b
Question 8	1 = 70.8, 2 = 63.8
Question 9	b
Question 10	£77.70
Question 11	a
Question 12	1 and 3
Question 13	2
Question 14	8 %
Question 15	b
Question 16	0.25

Answers to Audio Mental Arithmetic Tests

Practice Test 1

Practice	104
Question 1	£220.95
Question 2	23
Question 3	C
Question 4	25 %
Question 5	0.5
Question 6	1.5 m^2
Question 7	12
Question 8	35
Question 9	£22.50
Question 10	1530
Question 11	1 h 25 m
Question 12	920

Practice Test 2

Practice	48
Question 1	19
Question 2	104
Question 3	£1000.00
Question 4	1/6
Question 5	10:05
Question 6	200 km
Question 7	£6.00
Question 8	136
Question 9	23
Question 10	16
Question 11	70 %
Question 12	11:45

Practice Test 3

Practice	34
Question 1	10:50
Question 2	0.45
Question 3	£83.00
Question 4	12
Question 5	£12.00
Question 6	1 h 45 m
Question 7	65 %
Question 8	162
Question 9	£472.00
Question 10	242
Question 11	16
Question 12	36

Practice Test 4

Practice	1.32
Question 1	10:20
Question 2	7
Question 3	60
Question 4	£40.00
Question 5	12:05
Question 6	30 %
Question 7	1/12
Question 8	30
Question 9	14
Question 10	3.8
Question 11	£108.00
Question 12	12

Practice Test 5

Practice	28
Question 1	175
Question 2	28 %
Question 3	200
Question 4	7
Question 5	£140.00
Question 6	25 cm^3
Question 7	85 %
Question 8	55
Question 9	1/10
Question 10	38
Question 11	152
Question 12	5

Practice Test 6

Practice	2632
Question 1	£40.82
Question 2	255
Question 3	£13.00
Question 4	6
Question 5	60 %
Question 6	£95.00
Question 7	3/7
Question 8	14 h
Question 9	32
Question 10	63 cm^3
Question 11	15:30
Question 12	10 %

Practice Test 7

Practice	29
Question 1	60
Question 2	3/5
Question 3	20 m
Question 4	60 %
Question 5	173
Question 6	1.8 km
Question 7	£274.00
Question 8	£1665.00
Question 9	9
Question 10	42
Question 11	16:00
Question 12	£30.00

Appendix 1

Mathematical terms

Many of the questions in the Numeracy Skills Test require only a relatively basic level of mathematical knowledge but they do assume a familiarity with a number of mathematical terms. The most important of these are defined below.

1. Mean

The mean of a set of values is calculated by adding all the values together and dividing by the total number of values.

> **Example** A group of 12 pupils have the following absences in a term
> **6 7 8 9 10 12 13 14 14 14 17 20**
> The total number of absences is the sum of these numbers = 144
> Number of pupils = 12. Mean number of absences = 144 ÷ 12 = 12

2. Mode

The mode or modal number is the number that occurs most frequently in a set of values.
In the example above, three pupils have 14 absences. This is the number that occurs most frequently.
The mode is 14.

3. Median

The median is the middle value of a set of numbers when these are arranged in numerical order.

> **Example** A group of seventeen pupils score the following marks in a test
> **14 16 17 18 19 21 23 24 26 28 28 29 31 33 36 38 39**
> There are 17 numbers so the middle value is the ninth value. The median is 26 in this example

4. Range

The range is the difference between the lowest and highest values. In the above example, the lowest value is 14 and the highest value is 39. The range is 39 − 14 = 25.

5. Quartiles

These are defined in Chapter 2.

Units and Symbols

Some of the questions in the Numeracy Test require a response that incorporates units. Instructions will be given in the question and usually take the form of a direction such as 'Give your answer in kilometres' Some of the most frequently used units and their symbols are given below.

Unit	Symbol	Unit	Symbol	Unit	Symbol
kilometre	km	square centimetre	cm^2	gram	g
metre	m	cubic metre	m^3	hour	h or hr
centimetre	cm	litre	l	minute	m or min
mile	m	cubic centimetre	cm^3	second	s
square metre	m^2	kilogram	kg		

When answering questions it is not essential to include the unit, but if you choose to do so, give the correct symbol.

Some of the Numeracy Test questions use specific **mathematical symbols** – the ones you are likely to encounter are shown below:

    < less than   **>** greater than

Appendix 2

This answer grid is for the practice tests in Chapter 5 and two of the mental arithmetic tests on the CD.

Test Number		Test Number	
Mental Arithmetic questions		**Mental Arithmetic questions**	
Practice		Practice	
Question 1		Question 1	
Question 2		Question 2	
Question 3		Question 3	
Question 4		Question 4	
Question 5		Question 5	
Question 6		Question 6	
Question 7		Question 7	
Question 8		Question 8	
Question 9		Question 9	
Question 10		Question 10	
Question 11		Question 11	
Question 12		Question 12	
Written Questions		**Written Questions**	
Question 13		Question 13	
Question 14		Question 14	
Question 15		Question 15	
Question 16		Question 16	
Question 17		Question 17	
Question 18		Question 18	
Question 19		Question 19	
Question 20		Question 20	
Question 21		Question 21	
Question 22		Question 22	
Question 23		Question 23	
Question 24		Question 24	
Question 25		Question 25	
Question 26		Question 26	
Question 27		Question 27	
Question 28		Question 28	

This answer grid is for the remaining mental arithmetic tests on the CD.

Test number		Test number		Test number	
Practice		Practice		Practice	
Question 1		Question 1		Question 1	
Question 2		Question 2		Question 2	
Question 3		Question 3		Question 3	
Question 4		Question 4		Question 4	
Question 5		Question 5		Question 5	
Question 6		Question 6		Question 6	
Question 7		Question 7		Question 7	
Question 8		Question 8		Question 8	
Question 9		Question 9		Question 9	
Question 10		Question 10		Question 10	
Question 11		Question 11		Question 11	
Question 12		Question 12		Question 12	

Test number		Test number	
Practice		Practice	
Question 1		Question 1	
Question 2		Question 2	
Question 3		Question 3	
Question 4		Question 4	
Question 5		Question 5	
Question 6		Question 6	
Question 7		Question 7	
Question 8		Question 8	
Question 9		Question 9	
Question 10		Question 10	
Question 11		Question 11	
Question 12		Question 12	

Index

Notes

Notes